DONALD DEWAR ATE MY HAMSTER!

and other tales

A Selection of

RON FERGUSON'S

Columns from

The Herald

Northern Books
from Famedram

FROM THE SAME AUTHOR

GEOFF.
The life of Geoffrey M Shaw
"An excellent introduction to the life of the most truly good and best-loved man of his time."
LIFE AND WORK

Black Diamonds and the Blue Brazil
"If football is the working man's opera, then Ron Ferguson is the Puccini of his day."
SCOTTISH FOOTBALL HISTORIAN

ISBN 0905 489 616

Published by Famedram Publishers Limited AB41 9EA
Printed in Hungary

Contents

Foreword

by Harry Reid, editor of The Herald

It was nine years ago that I first became aware of Ron Ferguson's excellence as a writer. I was charged with "gutting" (as we call it in the trade) his biography of George MacLeod. We had done a deal with HarperCollins to present pre-publication extracts of this important book in *The Herald* over a period of several days.

Now the task of "gutting", or going through a text carefully to select appropriate and balanced extracts for publication in a newspaper, can be a pleasant journalistic chore or a nightmare. All depends on the quality of the text. One thing is certain: the "gutting" process tells you a great deal about the skills of the author concerned. You learn how his book has been put together. The extent to which he has, or has not, mastered his material and presented it sympathetically, fluently and intelligently. You get to know the text inside out. The author is left with few secrets to conceal from you.

On this occasion, the "gutting" was not just a pleasant chore, it was one of the brightest episodes in my journalistic career. I knew a little about Ron already; I knew of his Church of Scotland career, and his leadership of the Iona Community. What I did not know, till then, was that he was a consummate writer.

The control and sensitivity with which he dealt with MacLeod's teeming and turbulent life was extraordinary. Ron seemed just as at ease in the bourgeois West End of Glasgow in the early years of this century as he was in the poverty-stricken Govan of the 1930s, as at ease in the fashionable purlieus of Edinburgh in the 1920s as he was in the hell of the trenches during the Great War. And that was just the first half of George's career!

Such apparent ease can be deceptive. Easy reading, as someone once said, means damn hard writing. But there was more than literary skill, important as that is. There was a spiritual charge in the writing, a sense of the religious – in the best sense of the word – that was almost palpably numinous. The greatest Scottish churchman of the century had, in short, found the perfect, the ideal, biographer.

From then on, I was a committed fan of Ron Ferguson. It was a privilege for me when, in 1997, as editor of *The Herald,* I was able to hire him as a regular columnist for the paper.

But that's enough from me – let his words speak for themselves. Ron Ferguson cannot write a dull sentence. He can be very funny, and sometimes he's just a little vulgar. His prose is charged with genuine spiritual power.

You will enjoy the pieces featured in this book. You are in the presence of a master.

Introduction

Jean Rook, that doyenne of Fleet Street columnists, once wrote a piece suggesting that the Queen should pluck her eyebrows. The article produced such a disturbance in the breast of one reader that, unable to sleep, she got up at 2 am and hoovered the whole house in a fury.

It's a strange business, this writing a weekly column. Words tapped into a computer in Orkney and faxed straight from the northern machine into the *Herald* office in Glasgow appear in print in front of some 300,000 people within hours. At the breakfast table, or on the bus or train, readers flip through the pages, and make a quick decision on whether or not to read the words. By the next day, the sweated-over text is consigned to bin or fire.

My brief is to provide up to a thousand words each week on anything that comes into my small but perfectly formed heid. I usually lock myself away in a little eyrie looking out over Kirkwall – a curious window on the world – and dream. What normally happens is that the words and images of the week's news float through the mind, and connect up with life experiences, books, films, and conversations late into the night. Something inchoate forms, and soon stream-of-consciousness words are tumbling on to the laptop screen. As with a book, the piece is never "finished", only abandoned as the deadline looms.

I've never scratched around for things to say, never had "writer's block". You've got to be brilliant to suffer from that condition. (I'm reminded of the Orkney farmer who said, "We're no very intellectual here – that means we just have to use wir brains.") I enjoy writing, even against – especially against – the pressure of deadlines. It's how I unwind and relax, in the way that some people play golf or watch telly. The very act of producing a weekly column – with a wee photie of one's crazed physiognomy at the top of it – is, by definition, an egotistical thing to do. So is preaching, however much it is cloaked in the language of humility and inadequacy. It's better to put one's hands up and acknowledge this, then get on with it, even have some fun. There is only so much angst that readers and congregations can be expected to take. Journalists and ministers alike stand in need of regular absolution.

What is the job of the columnist? Peter Jenkins, that outstanding political commentator, said that columnists spent a great deal of their time reading the papers on behalf of their readers, trying to make a pattern out of a torrent of words. He added that the job of the columnist was to take an ego trip to entertain the readers, "preferably by annoying them, with strong opinions on each and every subject."

Columns are all about opinions, often instant opinions; and about judgments, often sweeping judgments. Consistency, mercifully, is neither required nor, indeed, expected. What the columnist tries to do is to get "inside" public events and discern a trend, a cultural shift, an emergent paradigm, an inner meaning: and then express these things in what is essentially a form of print entertainment, a piece of journalistic vaudeville. Whether the columnist succeeds or not is a matter for editors and readers to decide.

What is for sure is that the columnist will soon know about it. I have learned that there are a lot of *Herald* readers – and strong opinions – out there. The Kirkwall eyrie is no fortress; it is regularly invaded by mail, fax, telephone, e-mail. I stand accused of bias against Protestants, Catholics, humanists, the Labour party, the Tory party, the Scottish National Party, psychiatrists (all untrue), and also against

Rangers, Celtic, Rupert Murdoch, spin-doctors and television (guilty, your honour.) The most vicious letters are invariably those ending "Yours in Christ". Nobody can put the boot in the groin like an aggrieved Christian. Most of the messages that come in, though, are heart-warming, and often hilarious.

This column, I am told, can sometimes come between husband and wife, provoking arguments, possibly even manic hoovering. It has, I am very glad to know, caused embarrassing outbreaks of hysterical laughter in crowded commuter train compartments. Now and again it has expressed a point of view that someone has longed to see in print.

A column is not scripture. As the Australian writer, Phillip Adams, has put it, "The columnist is writing for an audience and a deadline, not for eternity." The nearest to eternity for a columnist is having a selection of pieces in book form, and I am pleased that Bill Williams of Famedram, who has published two of my previous books, has been so enthusiastic about publishing this anthology.

These pieces were all written during the course of the past two years, but are not in chronological sequence. They are largely printed here as they first appeared, though some dated references have been eliminated, and there has also been the odd piece of tidying up.

I would like to thank Harry Reid, not only for writing a generous foreword and for giving permission to use these pieces, but also for inviting me to contribute a regular column in the first place. Both Harry and executive editor Colin McDiarmid have been great sources of encouragement to me. I would also thank Bill McArthur from the island of Sanday, Orkney, for the cartoon on the cover and inside the book; Bill's brilliant cartoons grace the *Herald* every day, and his main political cartoon appears next to my own piece each week. I hope there will soon be a book of his art work.

Above all, I'd like to thank the readers of the *Herald*, to whom this book is dedicated. I hope those who buy this book will enjoy reading the articles as much as I did writing them.

RON FERGUSON
Kirkwall

DONALD DEWAR ATE MY HAMSTER!

He's a perpetually hungry man: but did he, or did he not, do the heinous deed of which he stands accused?? All will be revealed. At any rate, the heading shows the power of the meejah in this time of mighty changes in our land. Well, you're reading this, aren't you? After all, if the *Sun* could produce a six-foot-deep heading on its front page, FREDDIE STARR ATE MY HAMSTER! surely the demure *Herald* can produce something more modest about one of our own omnipresent cultural icons?

The heading isn't entirely misleading. This piece is about Scotland's Man of the Moment. It's also about one of my household pets. And a hamster with teeth-marks comes into the story. But are the teeth marks Donald Dewar's? Read on, MacDuff.

So, let's start at the beginning. We used to have a black labrador called Molly. She was a splendid, good-natured creature. She oozed unconditional love and forgiveness – a walking, wagging theological metaphor.

There were some complications. Our next door neighbour in Govan – where this riveting political tale is set – was also called Molly. This led to some interesting situations; for instance, when I went out into the street and called Molly in at night.

Molly liked to lie beside me on our hairy old couch (the dog, I mean, not the next door neighbour), and she did not care to surrender her special bit. Not even when the Shadow Secretary of State came to visit.

Enter Donald Dewar on left. He had come to converse with some friends in our house. Some of the most finely-honed minds in Europe - well, Govan - were assembled in our living room.

Mr Dewar chose his seat. On the hairy couch. Molly's seat. You get the picture? Others squeezed on to the couch as well.

This was something of a crisis for the dug.

Donald was talking about what Labour would do for the poor when it came into power. At that time, the prospect seemed very remote. Margaret Thatcher was into her second term, and Labour looked unelectable.

This most civilised of politicians raged against what he saw happening in our society. We were mesmerised as he waved his arms and spoke with passion. He articulated what seemed a far-off dream, of a Scotland with its own parliament, fighting a war against poverty.

Our eyes were fixed upon him. The dog had her eyes fixed upon the couch. She was totally focused. First one paw went on. Donald kept on talking. Then another paw. Then, a little bit of body, squeezed narrowly in between the Shadow Secretary and the person sitting next to him.

Have you noticed that dogs have an incredible ability to make themselves smaller, especially when they've done something wrong? Donald, listening to a questioner, moved further to the side. Molly was winning the battle for *lebensraum.* She sensed the man was in full flow, unable to notice what was happening right beside him.

It was our distinguished guest's turn to shrink. I saw what was happening, but dared not interrupt. Before my very eyes, the Shadow Secretary became smaller as Molly grew larger. She looked at me with her soft brown eyes.

Then she seized the moment. Suddenly, she insinuated herself fully on the couch, on *her* seat. Donald was marginalised, like the poor he was talking about. Perched he was, on the edge of the settee, still gesticulating. Hitting the ground talking? I didn't like to think of it.

Molly closed her eyes contentedly. Game, set and match to the dug.

I thought of all that this week when I saw a picture of Donald Dewar ensconced in his seat of power. As I looked at his face, I saw how much he had, in the intervening years, come to resemble our dog. Uncanny! What kind of political osmosis had happened during that fateful encounter on the couch in Govan?

But what about the hamster, you cry. Were the teeth marks Donald Dewar's?

Well I'll tell you. Our hamster used to run perpetually on a wheel, like a demented Calvinist on Ecstasy. As it did so, it was watched avidly by our cat, which had only one thing on its mind – meals on wheels. To move temptation out of the way, we put the hamster's cage on top of a wardrobe. The friendly feline sat there listening to the squeaking of the wheel, appealing to the heavens.

One day, when the roof of the cage was dislodged, the tiny kamikaze creature ejected itself like a pilot in distress, into the air and on to the floor, right beside the cat – which became at that precise moment a believer in God.

The only death-wish on a comparable scale that I have witnessed was when senior pin-striped lemmings came swarming over the Border before the last General Election to tell us that No, No, we couldn't have a parliament in Scotland even if we wanted one.

Anyway: the cat cheerfully observed the Big Mac it had ordered hitting the ground breathing. Muttering "for what we are about to receive.....", it sprinted downstairs, hamster in mouth. We chased it, in a scene reminiscent of Tam o' Shanter. In its fright, the cat dropped the terrified creature on the floor. It lay there quivering, teeth marks on its back.

The teeth marks were not Donald Dewar's. I now confess: the Gangling Scottish Gannet did not eat my hamster. The creature lived on – though its quality of life, as they say, wasn't great.

So, despite the rumours which circulate among grown men in Govan to this day, I hereby acquit the Secretary of State for Scotland.

I'm glad that his dream of a Scottish Parliament is no longer virtual reality. The Shadow has at last become substantial.

But what I remember most of all was what he said he'd do for the poor. Now strange things can happen to politicians when they become ensconced in seats of power, rather than perched on hairy old couches.

I could (almost) have forgiven the starving statesman if he had eaten my hamster. But not if he should eat his words.

Sliding doors of social exclusion

Down in London at the weekend to participate in a surreal World Cup writers' event, I went with my student daughter to watch a film, *Sliding Doors.* It features *Four Weddings and a Funeral* star John Hannah as a very personable Scot living in London, and it tells two different stories about the same people on a "What if?" basis.

The leading female character is unexpectedly fired from her job, and heads for home, early. In the first version of the tale, the sliding doors of the train close just before she can get on board. She then meets John Hannah on the later train, and a whole sequence begins to unfold. The director then rewinds the camera; this time our heroine prises open the sliding doors just before they close, and she gets home in time to find her partner in bed with his lover. The rest of the film is devoted to the differing consequences of the two distinct scenarios.

After the film, Fiona and I went to an Indian restaurant much frequented by her fellow music students. It's a delightful place; the food is delicious but inexpensive, the management gracious. We talked about the film we'd just seen, about the zany football event at the South Bank I'd been speaking at, and about my daughter's forthcoming recital.

As we talked we gradually became aware of the conversation from a table two along from ours in the crowded restaurant. Two men were seated across from one another, eating curry and drinking beer. They had started off fairly quietly, but as the evening had progressed, their jocular voices had become gradually louder, to the point at which we had begun to become aware of them. The accents were Scottish, from the west of Scotland.

More beer. The voices were becoming more difficult to ignore. In fact, they were downright obtrusive. Soon, it was fucking this, fucking that. Another glass. Bonhomie was giving way to something different, something a bit more edgy. The decibel levels went up to talk about "fucking Glenn Hoddle". The English, the two men observed to a bemused Indian waiter, were going to get banjoed in the World Cup. Cheers!

The men loudly inquired of the restaurant manager what his name was. Mr Hadji, they were told. "Well, Mr Hashish," shouted one, as the other laughed uproariously at his friend's rapier wit. Mr Hadji smiled benignly; then, with a mixture of charm and skill, he managed to escort the two clients gently towards the door. They went out, ready to harangue the English in the streets of London.

Bonnie Scotland, we'll support you ever more.

The interchange had a certain charmless familiarity about it. I've been there before, lots of times. The tiresome progression from generalised goodwill, to offensive loudness, to hostility, to menace, to aggression is no more appealing after the hundredth run through.

John Hannah, the brilliant Scottish actor from East Kilbride, now making it big in London: these two guys from the west of Scotland acting perfectly the parts of garrulous, obnoxious Scottish McPratts. What kinds of sliding doors have been operating in their lives? What if?

Wind back the film, and you're looking at confidence and lack of it. You're looking at the luck of the draw, the Great Lottery. It Could be You: on the other hand, it might not. Different genes, different sliding doors. If only.

It's not just about luck, though, or about great fingers pointing from the sky. Nor is it just about genes. It's also about choices, moral and cultural. It's about the kind of choices that the likes of John Hannah and the two drunk guys have made, but also about the political choices which have shaped the environments in which they have been brought up.

I know very little about the background of John Hannah, the rising Scottish film star. His family and community environment may have helped him or hindered him. He may have simply gone with the flow of a secure family life and education, or he may have had to struggle against the odds.

Nor do I know the backgrounds of the two Scottish football supporters in the restaurant. I would hazard a guess, though, that they grew up in an environment which did not support them well. They may have been part of a cultural food chain which gave them little personal nourishment. Domestic circumstances, environment and schooling may have combined to diminish what little confidence they had. Throw in excessive drinking and violence as a way of warding off melancholic fears of worthlessness, and the unlovable stereotype comes swaggering out into the streets. I may be wrong about these two men, but I doubt it. I've been there, seen it, too often, and I don't fancy the tee-shirt.

It is insecurity, not arrogance, which breeds aggressive "Wha's like us?" braggadocio. It's lack of confidence, not self-belief, which fuels the obnoxious racist rants. It is want of self esteem which produces the Scottish whine.

The Scottish cultural script has many attractive aspects. The generosity and boisterous passion seen, for instance, in the Tartan Army in France, and in the rapport between Scottish and Brazilian fans are immensely attractive.

But the Scottish tartan also has darker hues. Some of the patterns relate to geography and climate, some to the residual legacy of a baleful and melancholic theological emphasis on deep and abiding unworthiness.

There are new choices to be made, though, and Scotland is a new, as well as an old, territory. One doesn't have to sing cringe-making pseudo-anthems about proud Edward's army (oh, how we need these English enemies!) to want to rise up and be a nation of confidence, breadth of vision, generosity and tolerance.

Yes, now's the day, and now's the hour: to reinvent ourselves, to rewrite the national political and cultural script: and to prise apart the sliding doors of social exclusion.

Mobile phone is off the menu

Please raise a glass to one of the great heroes of the late 20th century, Mr Lawrence Clifford. The name may not be over-familiar to you, but he should be toasted in the very best of vino all over the country. I'll explain in a minute, but let me first digress.

I love travelling by train. Air travel has never appealed to me. Being over 6 feet tall, I find my chin on my knees a lot of the time. I also dislike the whole plastic flying culture, starting with the cheery announcements by the pilots ("This is your captain speaking. My name is Roger Arbuthnot, and sharing the flight deck with me is Flight Lieutenant Conrad Willis.") Frankly, I couldn't care less if it's Fat Bob who's flying the wretched machine, as long as he gets me there safely, on time.

(And why, after giving us their formal names, do the pilots say, "And Debbie will be looking after you in the cabin."? Debbie who? Why do the burdz not get their full names? And why are the stewardesses always so young and unlined, with understandably glazed smiles? If I'm going to tumble 10,000 feet in free-fall into the Pentland Firth, roaring for my mammy, I'd rather a mature woman with a lived-in face and stretch marks was doing the comforting. But that's between me and my therapist.)

Besides, the plane out of Kirkwall is a Shorts 326, one of those ugly garden sheds with wings stuck on them, palmed off to us by the wretched British Airways, a name reviled for its betrayal of the Highlands and Islands. The cabins are unpressurised, and by the time you're crossing over Wick your lugs are falling off with pain, your temple is throbbing, the cheery captain is giving you the totally pointless information that you're flying at 15,000 feet, you have a cup of something wet, along with food that is even less edible than the plastic container – and it's costing you £350 for the privilege of flying to Glasgow and not being able to hear again for a week. (Though here's a hot tip, free of charge. It was told to me by "Debbie": if the pressure is getting to your lugs, clamp a plastic tea cup over each auricle, and even though you will look like a manic Biggles all will be well. Remember, you read it first in this helpful and kindly column.)

I'm not very keen on bus travel, either (though, at least the driver doesn't announce, "This is your captain speaking; we're driving at 3 miles per hour through heavy traffic", and no one will smile at you pityingly and say "Have a nice day" as you lurch off the bus.) The main problem is that a normal human can't read on a bus without succumbing to life-threatening migraine after about five joogling seconds.

Cars are even worse. Not only can you not read, you're liable to be chased for miles by some finger-jabbing, starey-eyed maniac for the capital offence of being too slow in moving off at the last traffic lights.

No, it's the train for me. I love a long journey. You're away from the phone, you settle down with the newspapers and books, you watch the peasants happily working in the fields as you flash past, and you meditate benignly upon the world.

Until recently, that is. One day, I had to go from Edinburgh to London, and I looked forward to the journey with great anticipation. It was a pleasant day, and I had a cracking book with me. Oh, the bliss of it!

Then it started. First of all, someone calling himself the First Steward addressed us over the tannoy in feely-touchy newspeak. We were addressed as "customers" - why not "campers"? - and were instructed to have a nice day. Actually, I was having a nice day until this crazed therapist kept invading my space. Any minute now, and we'd be into group bonding exercises in the compartment. Could things get worse? Yes.

Ring, ring. Hello? Yes, Trevor here. I'm on the train to London. Yes, it's a lovely day.

Ring, ring. Hello? Yes, it's Alex. How are things back at the ranch? Everything OK? Will you put the dinner on for seven? Super! Cheers!

One of the great joys of train travel used to lie in getting away from the phone. Now the wretched instrument has invaded the train. The compartment was beginning to sound like a BT exchange. The incessant ringing and the high-decibel conversations were utterly intrusive. If the talk had been about an interesting undercover plot to frame Donald Dewar or something like that, it would have been worth putting down the book for five minutes just for the fun. But no: all we had were shouted banalities which simply served to validate the thesis that these miserable mobile phones actually microwave the brains of the people using them.

Just when there was a slight gap in the gormless phone chatter, our cheery First Steward would come on the tannoy to wish us good karma or something. For the first time in my life, I found myself longing for Debbie, the airborne garden shed, the cardboard food and the plastic cups over my lugs.

We are a nation in the grip of a terminal fear of silence. It's impossible nowadays to sit down in a restaurant, or go shopping, without ghastly muzak rotting the brain. You can't even have a haircut without it. And it's impossible to have five minutes of silence somewhere, anywhere, without some insensitive sod's mobile breaching the peace.

Which brings me back to one Lawrence Clifford, hero. The splendid man is a chef at the Gallery restaurant, Ipswich. He spends his time preparing good food, and he was annoyed, as were other diners, when a businessman's mobile kept going off, and the self-important highly-paid hooligan conducted tedious conversations at the top of his strangulated voice. When the offending man went to the toilet, Lawrence Clifford nipped in and removed the £250 mobile phone from the table, dipped it in batter, cooked it in boiling oil and served it to the owner with chips and salad.

Good on you, pal. It's fightback time – time to reclaim the day, the night, the airwaves, time for some anarchic street-compartment theatre of protest. Yes, raise a glass to Lawrence Clifford, freedom fighter. And if anyone is shouting at a restaurant near you, show him a copy of this article and enquire of him politely, "And how do you like your phone done, sir?"

More of the Ming Dynasty would do us no harm

He was a boyhood hero of mine. Thickset, a human bulldog, he would be prepared to die for the cause. A rough miner with huge hands, Alex Menzies knew what danger was, having worked underground since he was 15 years old.

Everyone in our town knew "Big Ming" and admired him. He resolutely refused to acknowledge defeat even when it stared him in the face – and it stared him in the face often, because he was Cowdenbeath football club's defiant centre half.

Big Ming belonged to the Desperate Dan school of Scottish manhood, with his diet of pies, fish suppers and beer. No one, but no one, could ever have any doubt about his loyalties. As Harry Ewing (later Lord Ewing) said of him, "If you were to cut Ming in half like a stick of Blackpool rock, he would have Cowdenbeath printed round his waist."

I have a clear image of Ming in a Cowdenbeath jersey. He would have stuck his head in a concrete mixer if there had been a ball in it. The big miner took no prisoners. Ming, like death, was a great leveller. Life-threatening injuries on Saturday afternoons – he once jumped off a stretcher to run back on the pitch and score a goal – would not prevent his appearance at his local hostelry on Saturday evenings.

I thought of Big Ming this past week, when I saw a photograph of Ally McCoist modelling one of the Versace suits with which the Rangers squad have been kitted out, and when I read of the plans of the Premier League clubs to break away from the rest.

Now this intrusion of sport into the centre pages may be jarring, but it provides a parable about the evolution of modern Scotland in all its contradictions. Big Ming, with an earring, strutting his stuff in Cowdenbeath High Street dressed in a Versace suit? I try to picture it, but there are some images which stubbornly refuse to form.

My earliest memory of Ming is his leading a Cowdenbeath team to Ibrox in the first leg of the quarter final of the Scottish League Cup. There were only two divisions then, and Cowdenbeath were in the lower division. The Rangers team they faced was one of the greatest in Ibrox history. It included Bobby Brown, Willie Woodburn, George Young, Tiger Shaw, Sammy Cox, Ian McCall and Torry Gillick. Sports writers protested that such a mismatch should even be allowed.

I have the hallowed cuttings in my house. The front page of the yellowed scriptures – Glasgow's *Evening News* – says it all: RANGERS GET A THRASHING. The young Cowdenbeath forwards pulled Woodburn and Young all over the place and impudently won 3-2, becoming the first ever Second Division side to beat Rangers at Ibrox. The newspaper reported that when the final whistle blew, Alex Menzies danced a Highland fling in front of the baying Ibrox punters. Danger was the big man's middle name.

The second leg was at Central Park four days later, when embarrassed Rangers came through to Fife to teach the part-time upstarts a lesson. There were 25,586 people – more than twice the population of the town – in the ground. I was there, perched high on my dad's shoulders. The first goal came in six minutes – for Cowdenbeath! The scorer was none other Big Ming. Desperate Gers pulled one back. With 13 seconds to go, Frank Armstrong, who had scored two goals at Ibrox, ignored Ming's shout, "Just kick it down Number 7 pit, Frank!" He tried to beat Geordie Young one time too many, lost possession, and Rutherford scored. Rangers got another in extra time. It was the first time I had seen grown men weep.

Those days are gone now, and in the past they must remain. The 1950s seem aeons away. Elite footballers in modern Scotland eat lettuce, drive free BMWs, flaunt jewellery, wear Italian designer suits. Most of the foreign players speak English better than Ming ever did. The football fans of the top clubs have changed, too. The loyalists who stood on the terracing in all weathers when the team were doing badly have been elbowed aside in a credit-card-carrying rush.

The top teams now wish to break away from the rest. Willie Miller, himself a former great defender-cum-referee, urged the smaller clubs to "set aside self interest" and vote for these changes.

Excuse me, Willie. Self interest? Are you suggesting that the top teams are acting out of idealism? One is reminded of Ralph Waldo Emerson's comments on a politician, "The louder he talked of his honour, the faster we counted our spoons."

The wee clubs are not destroying Scottish football. It is being seriously wounded by the already failed pursuit-at-any-price of a European chimera. Millions of pounds are being spent on foreign players – some of whom, at least, are expensive dumplings – instead of being invested in youth. This short-termism is lethal. The greedy emperor has no clothes.

The leaders should be cleaning up their own act and

asking questions such as: Why is it that top players and managers can treat signed contracts with contempt? Was Tommy Docherty right when he said, "Managers have to be cheats and con men – the only way to survive is by cheating"? Why is it that few Scottish clubs have proper training and coaching facilities? Why is it that when smaller clubs bring through youngsters, the big clubs can snap them up without a penny compensation?

There was a lot wrong with the world in which Big Ming flourished, and there is no point in romanticising it. But the seemingly unchallengeable movement towards the flash, finance-driven, ethics-free zone in which Paulo di Canio and Paul Gascoigne stamp their feet and get what they want cannot be the only model which is on offer.

As I sit in the new Alex Menzies (600-seater!) stand at Central Park, I reflect that a little bit of the Ming dynasty would do no harm in modern Scottish football. And in the meantime, the provincial clubs should keep counting their spoons.

Getting sex back on the tracks

When sex is good, said Groucho Marx, it's very good, and when it's bad, it's still pretty good. This, of course, is a man's view. Not every man's view, though. The Earl of Chesterfield once famously said of sex, "The pleasure is momentary, the position ridiculous, and the expense damnable."

What is for sure, though, is that since 1963 when, as Philip Larkin suggested, sex was invented, it has been the No.1 topic. A trawl through the newspapers on any given day reveals a very high proportion of stories about sex; and with films and television, there is no need to even bother to argue the case.

Sex has moved all the way from being forbidden to being compulsory. It has graduated from the closet to the living room – even, it seems, to the railway tracks. Last week, a train ran into an American couple who were having sex on the tracks. (Oh, what a perfect day! Did the earth move for you, darling, or was that a train which just ran over us?) Gives getting off at Haymarket a whole new dimension. Must have made a change from leaves on the track causing the delay.

The couple were not killed, though the man may now have a high-pitched voice. What is truly bizarre is that the injured pair are now suing the New York subway for $10m (which, by the way, is the sum which Monica Lewinsky is seeking from publishers for her memoirs of sunny days at the White House with Buffalo Bill.) Presumably the rail company were culpable for not having a sign saying "Sex on the tracks during rush hour is dangerous". It seems that litigation-happy Americans not only have the constitutional right to humph machine-guns around with them in case someone insults them at a party, but also to engage in sexual congress on the railway line as the 5.25 pm express hurtles down the track as well. Sleepers awake!

Could this madness ever happen in Britain? Well, yes. Take the story of everyday sensational folk which appeared in the *Herald* under the heading "BBC films couple having Viagra sex". The story reveals that the BBC have recorded a self-styled sex therapist, the wondrously-named Tuppy Owen, making love with her partner, Anthony, hours after he had popped a Viagra pill, for BBC2's Modern Times series. Tuppy, who is apparently being paid as a "consultant" for the programme, is the author of such modern literary classics as *Take Me, I'm Yours* and *The Sex Maniac's Diary.*

You couldn't make this stuff up. The gorillas have finally taken over the monkey house. Yet it is announced in BBC po-faced tones, saying that "It is clear that the introduction of Viagra into the UK market will make it one of the biggest stories of the year." As if on cue, Mrs Mary Whitehouse rushes in with a demand that the programme be banned, and the producers, enjoying the predictable publicity which the news was bound to generate, can adopt the spurious pose of injured defenders of the truth. No mention of the fact that Viagra, the wonder drug, will raise their limp ratings.

Is there less exploitation, and more honesty about sex nowadays? The received wisdom needs to be challenged. The days when sex was a taboo subject have certainly long since gone. Even young children have been made sexually aware. Primary-school kids talk of condoms as if they were the latest multi-flavoured chewing gum, and show knowledge of exotic sexual practices unknown to most of their grandparents, if not their parents.

Sex is talked about at length, at the top of the voice, everywhere. But as religious puritanism has been steadily abandoned, it has been replaced by a new and strange kind of omnipresent secular perfectionism.

Puritanism, said H.L. Mencken, is based on the fear that somewhere someone is enjoying himself. The new inverted sexual Puritanism is based on the fear that somewhere someone is doing it better. Hence the rash of sex manuals, showing techniques and positions which would appear to require degrees in plumbing, engineering, and aerodynamics. Tallulah Bankhead, who knew a thing or three about such matters observed, "I've tried several varieties of sex. The conventional position makes me claustrophobic. And the others either give me a stiff neck or lockjaw." (It was the same lady who famously instructed, "I'll come and make love with you at five o'clock. If I'm late, just start without me.")

Performance anxiety is the new paralysing tyranny. This is a very strange form of liberation. It is the dread of failing the Great Performance Exam which is apparently fuelling the world-wide stampede for Viagra. The pill is a boon for those who are impotent, but all the evidence indicates that the reason it is the fastest-selling legal drug in history has more to do with sexual pressures. Men are literally dying for it. Swallowed without medical checks, as it often is, the little blue miracle pill has the potential to kill. The death toll in America is already close to 100. The torrents of the Viagra Falls will heal some, and sweep many away.

Sex can be ecstatic, disappointing, enriching, destroying, tedious and pleasurable. It can be a source of great pain and great joy. It has the capacity to convey tenderness and brutality, passion and exploitation. It can be a source of life, and death. It is both ennobling and truly preposterous, rightly the subject of raunchy and funny jokes. What it cannot do is bear the weight of ultimate meaning.

The current wall-to-wall sexualisation of society is in danger of turning love-making from something essentially intimate and private and relational into a grotesque global television game show for voyeurs.

The perfectionist-piston sexual ideology adds yet another competitive strain to an already driven culture. Remember the salutary fate of one of Woody Allen's typically anxious characters – "I finally had an orgasm, and then my doctor told me it was the wrong kind."

Waves which threaten the upturned boats

Where will power really lie when the new Scottish parliament hits the ground blethering? Will Edinburgh be where it's at, or will London reign supreme? Or even Brussels?

The death of Tiny Rowland is a timely reminder of other realities – shadowy unaccountable global powers which can render democratically elected governments as toothless as a local council.

At his height, Tiny Rowland had the leaders of several African countries feeding from his outstretched paw. As head of Lonrho, he made his name as a rapacious entrepreneur. As one commentator put it: "He moved boldly in, treating the continent like one vast car-boot sale."

Rowland was totally focused on making money. He knew how to bribe and manoeuvre his way to power. He once said famously, "There's not a single man I could not buy. Every man has his price. The definition of an honest man is when his price is too high."

Like most tycoons, he was fascinated by newspapers. Donald Trelford, editor of *The Observer,* recalled spending a summer on the new proprietor's yacht in the Mediterranean. "There would be the most fantastic scenery, but Rowland would simply stand staring at the phone, waiting for it to ring. When it did ring it would always be Nelson Mandela, or the president of Kenya, or the head of Mossad or someone like that. He was the centre of this most amazing international network."

In 1992, "the unacceptable face of capitalism" was rescued by a huge loan from Rowland's pal, Colonel Gaddafi. Accused of outrageous behaviour, the bold Rowland said bluntly, "Don't talk to me about morality. I pay my taxes here."

The one man who managed to outwit him was Mohammed al Fayed. The phoney Pharaoh has been as ruthless in his business dealings as he has been in peddling conspiracy theories about the death of Diana and Dodi. The two rival wheeler-dealers have inflicted a fair bit of damage in their time.

Consider also that other international tycoon, Robert Maxwell. Another ruthless man devoted to money, power, status and influence, he was also fascinated by newspapers. His performance over the short-lived *Sunday Standard* and his company's ownership of the *Daily Mirror* and its sister paper the *Daily Record* are not remembered with affection in Scotland. Maxwell's resources enabled him to extend his malign influence to different parts of the world. Like other tycoons, he protected himself from too close scrutiny by the media. He threw around libel writs like confetti, and it was this power which enabled him to filch much of the Mirror pensioners' money.

And Rupert Murdoch. His assets are estimated at £7bn. The Australian's reach extends around the globe. Again, he is fascinated by media power, owning 20th Century Fox, HarperCollins, BSkyB, television interests in China, *The Sun*, and *The Sunday Times*. He deals coldly and quickly with anyone who cuts across his financial interests. Ask Chris Patten. The reclusive Barclay brothers, who own *The Scotsman* and *The European* newspapers, are said to be worth at least £50m.

Then there is Bill Gates, the richest man in the world, whose global Microsoft empire is all-conquering. Most of us who use computers are dependent on his ubiquitous software, and he has a huge stake in the burgeoning world-wide Internet system of communications.

The power and influence of these wealthy, highly-focused and ruthless individuals - and there are many more out there - is enormous. When you add in the huge multi-national companies like Coca Cola, MacDonalds, and Nestles, plus the big international financial players, you are talking about very substantial global power - not just in economic, but in cultural terms. The new cultural imperialism no longer involves a single dominant country sending out traders and missionaries; it is a pervasive mindset which affects us all. It is in the air we breathe and the air-waves we tune in to, part of a global consensus trance.

Since the collapse of socialism in Europe, the victory of international capitalism has been loudly celebrated. The Labour Party in this country has joined in the singing and dancing. They would do well to remember the aphorism that he who marries the spirit of the age will be a widower for a long time. To trumpet the triumph of capitalism as irrevocable is to lose sight of history. A world economic slump and stock exchange collapse, followed by a global recession, would lead to a radical re-assessment. Boom-and-bust is the nature of the capitalist beast.

State-controlled socialism is a god that has failed, miserably. As Nobel prize-winner C.F. von Weizsacker has put it: "The sin of modern capitalism is cynicism, and the sin of socialism is lying." Hence the search for a Third Way. The trouble is that there is nothing so far in the Blair project which suggests anything fundamentally serious beyond the warm words. There is no hint of an emerging political philosophy that will even begin to tackle the issue of unaccountable global power. Who, for instance, will challenge what the western powers are doing to the Third World?

The political body language gives the game away. Blair has felt it necessary to cosy up to Rupert Murdoch and Bill Gates to keep the great men "on side". The smiling lamb has obligingly lain down with the lion in the great Blair eschatological vision. The trouble is that it is in the nature of the lion to rip the lamb apart when it shows the slightest sign of growing up, of ceasing to be a pet.

The question of where real power will lie, in the absence of radical economic change, is at the crux of the great millennial future. When the economic and political waves hit the Scottish shore, what are the chances of the upturned boats of Holyrood being able to weather the storm?

Affluenza: the long good buy

Sometimes it's hard to be a man. The research proves it. Us poor wee souls of the now-weaker sex get stressed out whenever we step inside a shop. Blood pressure rises, the fight-or-flight system goes into overdrive, heart palpitations begin: the symptoms are akin to those exhibited by fighter pilots going into a danger area. The advent of Christmas is male panic-attack time. I write this in the sure and certain knowledge that the ladies out there will be entirely sympathetic to our plight, and ready to administer soothing and kindly balms.

Research also shows that a high proportion of women prefer shopping to sex. (I forget which of the current 325 television documentaries about sex produced the statistics.) Apparently, if they're going to be subjected to an uncomfortable, eye-gouging, frustrating experience, most women would prefer it to be in the bargain basement at Marks & Spencers than at hame with wee Malky on Viagra. Aye, it's hard to be a man in these testing times.

Here are some welcome tidings from America: too much shopping can endanger everybody's health, male and female. The need to buy more and more is apparently causing an illness which is now officially described as "Affluenza". Dr Richard Swenson of Colorado says that we are all suffering from "possession-overload", and it is making us ill. The symptoms are anxiety, depression, insomnia, fluey-feelings, headaches and continual tiredness.

Affluenza, it seems, is increasingly making its presence felt in Britain. It will soon be showing at a hospital near you. Here are some interesting facts from across the pond.

- The average human being receives 3,000 marketing messages a day.
- By the time you are 21, you will have seen or heard a million advertisements.
- By the time you pop your clogs, you will probably have spent a whole year of your life watching television commercials.
- Americans spend six hours a week shopping, and only 40 minutes playing with their children.

We inhabit a consuming culture. Well, a third of the world does. Confronted with a choice between the bare shelves of Moscow and the well-stocked superstores of our Scottish cities, no one in their right mind would choose the former Soviet option. But here is another illuminating piece of research. A study a few years ago showed that there was a clear correlation between increased wealth and happiness in Third World countries, but there was no such correlation in the West. In the more affluent parts of the world, increased wealth does not bring increased happiness, unless, that is, you inhabit the poorer parts of the wealthy world.

Americans buy twice as much as they did in 1957, but rate themselves as only half as happy now as they were then. Even allowing for romanticising about the good old days, and that other factors come into play, the figures are significant.

If you are poor, even a modest increase in resources will increase your happiness levels. It stands to reason that if you are perpetually anxious about survival, personal happiness is much less liable to flourish. But if you are secure and well-off, a rise in your income will not necessarily increase your happiness quotient.

This was brought home to me personally this year, when visiting India. I wouldn't consider myself particularly well-off in this country, but in India I felt like a millionaire compared to most people. In Calcutta I saw men pulling other human beings on rickshaws for a few rupees, and witnessed the large number of people sleeping out on the pavements. An incremental rise in their living standards would certainly raise both health and happiness levels dramatically.

It seems that once we pass the "enough" level on the income graph, rises in income don't make much difference to human satisfaction. In fact, paradoxically, anxiety, boredom and worry often increase. Research published this week showed that well-off 25-year-olds today are ten times more likely to suffer from depression than their grandparents did.

Yet in the run-up to Christmas, we are bombarded with messages urging us to consume at ever-higher levels. The Christmas rush largely consists of well-off people anxiously searching for fairly expensive presents for other well-off people. The ever-powerful reach of television ensures that people on low incomes are under severe pressure to buy expensive items for children who will be pilloried if they aren't wearing the latest brand names. Our standard of living is predicated on perpetual growth in the economy: yet all the indicators tell us that ever-increasing consumerism is steadily destroying our planet. A San Francisco research group, called Redefining Progress, has done the sums: if the whole world were to consume at the rate of the average American, another three planets would be needed! Yet such is the power of advertising that the lifestyle of the average American is held up as the ideal to which most people should aspire.

The affluenza epidemic, then, is not just debilitating; it

has terminal consequences. The large economic and environmental writing is on the global wall, but we would rather not read it.

The combination of international business interests, global communications and hype is a lethal one. It is very, very hard to stand against its power. Its images are pervasive. Its presuppositions are in the air we breathe. Its short-term definitions of the good life dominate current political discourse: the major political parties accept the underlying, unspoken assumptions of this ideology, and would be swept into oblivion if they were to stand on a platform challenging them.

It is ironic that Christmas – a festival celebrating the birth of a child in poverty, one who grew up to challenge the religious and political power structures of his day – is the festival which has been most obviously co-opted by the dominant consumer ideology.

AlterNativity. What do you get at Christmas for the man who has everything? A doomsday clock.

Blood on our hands

There he was, naked except for a strip of cloth, alone, arms outstretched, a forlorn and abandoned figure. And he was dead, the victim of the fury of an uncontrollable mob. I don't remember his name, but his image is imprinted on my memory.

He was a young man who had hardly learned how to live. He was, as he understood it, only doing his duty. That duty took him to a funeral, to help keep public order. There was a disturbance, then shots, and the crowd of mourners pursued the young man and trampled him to death. Then they went home.

The young British soldier was a victim. Joining up had seemed a better choice than being on the dole. He understood little of the Irish troubles. He would save up some money, see out his contract, marry and settle down perhaps, bring up children. It had seemed a good choice at the time. Now, he was stretched out, cross-shaped on the green cemetery turf, a Good Friday image, killed in a blood-lust righteous frenzy.

Some years before, bodies of dead and wounded people had lain on the ground. A priest, holding aloft a white handkerchief, was administering the last rites to a unarmed dying man, slain in an angry hail of bullets. This was a Sunday sacrifice. Bloody Sunday.

It is highly symbolic that the Irish peace process has

come to a crux on the brink of the black day we call Good Friday, the day of suffering and abandonment.

There are people who will argue that this conflict has really nothing to do with religion, that it is all a matter of economics and politics. The people who say this are often churchmen, seeking to absolve the churches of blame for the Troubles. It will not wash, not on Good Friday, nor any other day.

Though the struggle is not just about religion, religious identity is at the heart of it. And behind the struggles in Ireland lie the sins of the churches, like open wounds. This day, above all days, is not a time for evading truth.

To understand the roots of the Troubles, it is necessary to go back to the Reformation. Many who look at the world through Roman Catholic – and therefore limited – spectacles, will interpret that historical cleavage as the result of pig-headed, self-indulgent rebels putting themselves before the good of the universal Church.

Many who look at the world through Protestant – and therefore limited – lenses will see the Reformation as a glorious time when heroic people stood up for the truth, in the face of a corrupt hierarchy with its corporate hearing-aid switched off.

Many who look at the world through humanist – and therefore limited – prisms, will dismiss all religion as fantastic talk.

It is heartbreaking to read the documents of the time. What is clear is that that there was a stage when the looming tragedy could have been averted. What was required on both sides was humility, listening and faithful action. Some of the great scholars of the Church, such as Erasmus, did their best to mediate. But stubbornness, pride, and power play won the day. Once they were rebuffed, the leaders of the reform movement, instead of sticking it out, walked out of the peace talks and formed their own churches. Their hierarchical opponents refused to look at any peace plan other than submission.

Thus there were two "sides", excommunicating each other, producing more and more extreme theological definitions. The Reforming Catholics, on a tide of popular enthusiasm and abetted by political princes who saw advantages in schism, set up alternative churches. The Roman Catholic Church, in reaction, became much more authoritarian, putting itself out of touching distance of the burgeoning reform movement. The cry, on both sides, was "No Surrender."

The rest is poisoned history. The story of Ireland is a particularly extreme acting out of the tragedy, with divided communities telling and re-telling only their own versions of history, often full of hatred.

The leaders of the divided communities in Ireland are today being called upon to help each other get out of prison. That requires humility, listening, imagination and courage. It is very hard for any of us to stand outside of our traditions, adjust our lenses and dare to see the world in a new way.

Those of us in the churches are in no position to preach reconciliation while we live division. For the churches to demand imaginative and courageous action from Irish political leaders and berate them for their failures is simply not on. To applaud deadlines, and encourage Sinn Fein and the Unionists to sit in locked rooms until a solution is found is one thing. But with the second millennium looming, where are the Church leaders who are prepared to set themselves a similar timetable for an historic and courageous imaginative leap? (This is exactly the process by which the historic church creeds were hammered out.) The churches need to be freed from their tribal historical prisons as well.

Good Friday in Ireland: the passion is set to continue,

peace process notwithstanding.

Easter Sunday in Scotland: passion of a different kind. A strangely restless nation, which is increasingly saying "a plague on all your ecclesiastical houses" – and which would not allow its football team to play later in the day of Diana's funeral – will settle down to watch a football match which the real god, commerce, has dictated will be held on the ancient holy day of resurrection. At the shrine called Ibrox, songs of religious hatred will cascade down from the stands.

As of old, the Cry will be No Surrender. Young victims will continue to die, cruciformed. And we in the churches, with our finery and fine words, custodians of a religion with an inherent capacity for exquisite beauty and transcendent human glory, have blood on our hands.

The batty realm of Psychobabylon

It had to be the story of the week. The inquiry into the running of Asworth Hospital was told that a resident psychologist, who is an expert in anger management, completely lost the heid one day and chased two of his colleagues down the hospital corridor before assaulting them.

(Hey! Who is that grizzly bear chasing two doctors down the corridor, shouting and swearing? Why, that's the anger manager! Just imagine what he's like when he's not managing his anger!)

This is a delicious story because so much of the psychological world today is wondrously po-faced, and takes itself very, very seriously. (So, too, does the world of religion: here's another cheery story of the week. It comes from Nebraska, USA. Police in Lincoln County were called in after two Bible salesmen were found duelling with baseball bats in a bitter turf war. Asked to comment on the fight, the Bishop of Nebraska threatened to "nut" any journalist who came near him. It looks as if the good bishop is a candidate for anger management counselling – if he can find an anger expert who isn't busy nutting his colleagues in encounter groups.)

We live in a batty wee world, one which is awash with experts in counselling. There must be at least three counsellors to every normal human being. After every incident, major or minor, counselling appears to be available. We are a nation in therapy.

In a plane crash? Post-trauma stress counselling is on offer. Forgot to post the winning football pools coupon? The Stress Liaison officer is at your door. Suffering from piles? The Haemorrhoids Hang Loose Support Group is for you. A friend recently went to a vet's community open day: naturally, pet-death bereavement counselling was on the menu. How did we all manage before?

The number of seriously dysfunctional people trying to mend other people's lives is enormous. I have known a lot of weird people in my time, and a suspiciously high proportion of them seem to be social workers, counsellors or clergy.

I well remember a long conversation on Iona with RD Laing, the great psychiatrist. Eminent and brilliant though he was, the dear man was daft as a brush. Takes one to know one, I suppose. As we walked along the island coastline, he expounded his extraordinary theory that people should run around at night instead of going to bed. He backed this up by running around the Iona machair at full moon, baying; then he lay outside the abbey, moaning. Apart from that, he was quite normal. I decided not to share my midlife crisis with him, and counted my blessings instead.

It's all very strange. Western Europe has been in the process of distancing itself from organised religion over many decades. The reasons for this are complex. One reason is the impact of science on the religious world view. Yet what has taken religion's place is not rationality, but therapy. Welcome to Psychobabylon!

Any representative of religion gets a serious grilling these days – a back-to-the-wall, sweat-running-down-the-face kebabbing – but for some reason the new therapeutic gurus are treated with breathless awe. No TV or radio programme, it seems, is complete without a word of wisdom from a counsellor with some imposing title or other. We are being bombarded with mind-rotting psychological mince, most of which makes "Late Call" seem like the intellectual high-point of European civilisation.

We are exhorted to Search for the Hero Within, or seek New Power through Colonic Irrigation. You're useless if you can't Get in Touch with your Cosmic Memory. You can even work off your double chin with a workout at the "chin gym".

Don't get me wrong. Wise counselling at the right time can do a lot of good. Like other things, it can help us human beings get through some rough patches. "I am for everything that helps anyone through the night," said the late Frank Sinatra, "whether it is prayer, a sleeping pill, or a bottle of whisky." There are some tremendously good counsellors around, and they have saved quite a few lives. But this counselling thing has become big business. A lot of bucks change hands. (Know why a psychiatrist is called a shrink? Because that's what he does to your wallet. You don't believe in shock therapy? Wait till you see the size of your bill.)

The whole world of therapy is exploding, and there are a lot of crazy people out there offering advice. There is apparently nothing to stop anyone setting up as a counsellor, putting some mickey mouse initials after their name, messing up your life, then charging you a fortune.

The language of Psychobabylon is pervasive. Let it all hang out. Tell it like it is. Where are you coming from? Let me share this with you. Will you stop acting out and start relating? What's the psychological pay-off ? Stop being anally-retentive and take responsibility! (How many counsellors does it take to change a light bulb? Three, but the light bulb has to want to change.)

In the unaccountable realm of Psychobabylon, no batty cliché is left unspoken, no colon left unplumbed, no wallet left undamaged. The emperor's clothes, though, are a bit threadbare, even though they're very expensively priced. Only Rikki Fulton could do this justice.

We're all affected by the language. In fact, I was going to tell you where I'm coming from, but I'm actually just going – very quickly. I was intending to do a bit of deep sharing with you, but two starey-eyed bible salesmen with baseball bats are running towards me, pursued by chequebook-waving sweating journalists, followed by a furious bishop, who's looking over his shoulder at a berserk anger management consultant. These life-menders look seriously dangerous.

You'll find me quivering in the chin gym, pretending to do face press-ups. With a bit of luck I'll quickly get in touch with my Inner Hero. The pyschological pay-off? Survival. Have a deeply meaningful day.

Oh, the light of my life

The summer light in Orkney is translucent, ethereal. At 11pm it is still brightish. I love these long evenings when the wind drops, and everything goes still. The waves are lapping gently against the boats. At times like this Orkney seems like the Garden of Eden.

That was how one of Orkney's favourite sons, Edwin Muir, saw it in certain moods. As he looked from his native island of Wyre, he reflected:

One foot in Eden still, I stand
And look across the other land.

It's easy to see why artists have flocked to this northern archipelago. They have tried to capture the changing light in their landscapes and seascapes. Dr Stanley Cursiter, a Kirkwall lad who became the Queen's Limner and Painter in Scotland, is only one of many who have been entranced by the quality of the light.

On fine summer evenings, the Viking St Magnus Cathedral stands bathed in sunshine, its red and yellow sandstone soft and welcoming. The Cathedral is itself a festival in stone. The spectacular contemporary stained glass window at the west end of the nave, unveiled in 1987 to mark the 850th anniversary of the founding of the Cathedral, has light as its theme. The window uses various ancient and modern Orkney motifs – Maeshow, a fish, the Ring of Brodgar, the Flotta flare, and the omnipresent corn.

In the mornings, the blue glass dominates, but the afternoon sun sets fire to the central golden circle and showers radiance into the nave.

Orkney weddings are normally held on summer evenings. The soft sunlight, streaming through the kaleidoscopic prism of the west window, magically transfigures strong Orcadian farming brides into mysterious Nordic princesses.

This is the season of visitors. The city and royal burgh of Kirkwall is thronging with people from all over the world. There is a veritable Babel of tongues - Norwegian, French, German, American, Japanese.

On a day like today, people become smitten with the islands. Many proclaim a determination to return to live - and a few do, fleeing the busy south, crossing the Pentland Firth accompanied by a goat, looking for the simple life. Ah, but only if it were so simple. The shadow, as always, crosses the Garden of Eden. As the season changes, darkness and light intermingle, like wheat and tares. Edwin Muir again:

The world's great day is growing late,
Yet strange these fields that we have planted
So long with crops of love and hate.
Time's handiworks by time are haunted,
And nothing now can separate
The corn and tares compactly grown.

Towards winter, after a fleeting autumn. The days become shorter. The winds howl. Some people suffer from S.A.D. - Seasonally Affective Disorder - a depression caused by lack of light. The summer optimism has evaporated.

Living on an Orkney croft in January is not a simple life. This is when the visitor with the goat heads back, older and wiser, to the bright lights and the busy city. Urban life seems not so bad.

The reality is that an island is the worst place to escape to: islands are by definition insular, and there is no escape. You still have to face yourself, and the self you face in North Ronaldsay is the same self you despaired over in London or Glasgow. There is no return to innocence, to the Garden of Eden. There is no way back.

The armorial weed in stillness bound
About the stalk; these are our own.
Evil and good stand thick around
In the fields of charity and sin
Where we shall lead our harvest in.

Yet the darkness produces great art, too. Out of depression and blackness, out of the shadow self, out of a sense even of the absence of God, great music and poetry and drama, deep in the soul, spring. The artist reaches for the darker colours of the palette. Duncan Maclean sits in Stromness, watching the words of his next novel on a screen before him. Peter Maxwell Davies walks around his cottage at Rackwick Bay, high above turbulent seas, then writes down turbulent notes.

Yet still from Eden springs the root
As clean as on the starting day.
Time takes the foliage and the fruit
And burns the archetypal leaf
to shapes of terror and of grief
Scattered along the winter way.

Then slowly, Spring. There are days when the gales may reach 120mph, and you know you are in a wind, not the wee breezes that southerners complain about. It was said of the town of Moose Jaw in Saskatchewan that one day the wind stopped and all the inhabitants fell down. For Moose Jaw, read Kirkwall.

St Magnus Cathedral now stands as a great defiant rock, a shelter in the storm.

I love the turbulence and the passion of the seas, the conflict, the clashes of colours, then the peace after the storm. No. Forget passive Eden. Keep the illusory simple life. Welcome complexity, subtlety, grace.

What had Eden ever to say
Of hope and faith and pity and love
Until was buried all its day
And memory found its treasure trove?
Strange blessings never in Paradise
Fall from these beclouded skies.

"Live in Orkney," wrote Eric Linklater, "and you know the meaning of summer, the meaning of winter. The year is a living thing, and you live with it. As the months lighten, you pass from the extravagant roughness of a limitless ocean to – on occasional days – the idyllic beauty of life in the midst of a sleeping sea. Your are intimately concerned with nature and the procreant forces of the earth. You may have been heroic under the pressure of winter; you will now be happy in the benison of summer."

Yes, the summer again. This is a benediction of a day – enjoy it while it is here. Did I ever tell you how beautiful Orkney is in the summer? How exquisite the light is?

Perils of the ploy named Sue

Here is a solemn health warning: please read this column from the top. If you start from the bottom and read upwards, it will be much more difficult for you. So don't say you haven't been telt. If you try to sue, my lawyers are waiting, expensively. I have instructed them to be merciless.

The reason for this disclaimer is an article in the *New Scientist,* which reveals how companies nowadays are stating the obvious on packets. For instance, did you know that the electrical firm, Rowenta, puts a notice on its new iron, "Do not iron clothes on body"?

I am devastated by this warning. I much prefer to iron my suit when I'm wearing it. It gives me that certain "lived-in" look which drives women crazy. The sensation of ironing my shirt while it's on my body is very heart-warming – I find it quite difficult, though, to iron the back of the shirt, as my arms aren't quite long enough.

The kind people at Sainsbury's have a message, apparently, on each 500g packet of peanuts. It says, solemnly, "contains nuts". Well, I'm really glad to know that. I might have thought I was eating pan drops with salt sprayed on them.

An American airline prints on its packet of peanuts a message which reads, "Instructions: open packet, eat contents." It's worth reading that sentence again: it contains information that will help you get through to the next Millennium. Isn't it great we've got these people looking after us? Otherwise, we might be tempted to eat the packet and spit out the contents. The packet, in fact, might be more nutritious.

Now, here's a real beezer, one which makes the previous messages look as if they were composed by Einstein. In America, there are stickers on the wing mirrors of bikes and cars saying, "Remember – objects seen in mirror are behind you." Honest – not a word of this is being invented. You see, you might think the objects you are seeing in your mirror are in front of you. If you actually think that, you shouldn't be driving a car. In fact, you shouldn't be allowed out your hoose at all, because you might kill the rest of us.

There's more, there's more. In America, an insect spray informs "kills all insects", and adds a warning, "harmful to bees." Just as well bees can read, otherwise they could be in serious trouble.

Here's another cracker. A Swedish chainsaw packet warns, "Do not try to stop chain with hands." I must say, that of all the things I have ever been tempted to do, stopping a chainsaw with my hands is not one of them. Now these Nordic misanthropes have put the notion into my head. From now on, every time I see a chainsaw at full blast, I will have to fight a battle with my Inner Eejit. I shall wreak vengeance by attacking every Volvo I see. Britain is not short of warnings. The message on Marks & Spencer's bread and butter pudding lets you know, "Take care – product will be hot after heating." Hot after heating? How can this possibly be?

Here's another piece of sensational information. There is a mixture called Nytol which is designed to help people sleep. The pack contains the terrifying warning, "May cause drowsiness." The last thing you want when you desire sleep is to feel drowsy, eh?

Boots cough syrup for young children advises, “Do not drive car or operate machinery. Avoid alcoholic drinks.” Foreign products have the usual problems with translation. A Korean kitchen knife has the message – “Warning – keep out of children.” Except, presumably, children high on Boots cough syrup, driving a car, and not knowing that the objects in their mirror are behind them. It’s a frightening wee world we live in, but this column is here to protect you.

Why is all this essential advice coming our way? The reason that in America, people sue at the slightest provocation. Do you remember the woman who put her poodle in the microwave to dry it? Scary. What is even more scary is that she sued the manufacturers – and won. You see, they had failed to put a notice on the microwave saying that you shouldn’t dry your dug in it. There are lawyers specialising in this stuff, and they are very, very rich.

Will the *Herald* have to put a bit on the front page warning readers not to eat the paper for their breakfast? Will bathroom mirrors have a sign saying that the scary person approaching you (from the front) is really your good self?

Enough of this consumer-neurotic western madness. For the next three weeks, this great and mighty column will come to you from India. No expense is spared so that you, dear readers, may have the most up to date intelligence from around the globe.

I look forward to the flight, especially to eating the cellophane wrapped around the peanuts. So, the next column will come to you from Calcutta: unless, that is, KLM have omitted to paint a warning on the wing: “Do not walk on this wing while the plane is flying at 30,000 feet.”

I shall try to avoid the children's cough mixture, especially while flying the plane when the pilot has a break. I will avoid any sleep-inducing mixture, in case it makes me drowsy. And I do hope they have an iron on the plane, so that I can defiantly take the creases out of my dhoti while I am wearing it.

Oh dear: I do hope the pilot has got a sticker on his wing mirror warning him that the objects he sees in it are behind him, not in front of him.

See you soon. I hope.

The success addict at Number Ten

Tony Blair, don't'cha just love him? Flashing teeth, all-singing all-dancing all-action premier, riding high in the popularity polls, strutting his stuff on the world stage, Superman, Batman (with his ever-mischievous pal, Robin) – what a guy! He's what the ancient Sufis would have called a "right performer". You get my point. No? Then let me explain.

The Sufis came to the fore in the Middle Ages, part of a revival in the theology and devotion of Islam. Nowadays, of course, Islam gets a bad press in the West. The public spotlight is usually on its harsher side, its hands-cut-off-for-thieving and lugs-lopped-off-for-overhearing aspect (though Christianity has done its fair share of chopping, torching and gouging in the name of the Lord.)

The high culture of Islam was a brilliant achievement. The Sufis developed a mystical theology and practice which was sublime, sophisticated, and inclusive. They also, apparently, developed a psychology of the personality which was picked up early this century by that Georgian genius-cum-charlatan, George Ivanovich Gurdjieff. Eventually, the teaching was encountered by American Jesuits and is now widely used in America and Britain as a tool for spiritual direction.

The system is called the Enneagram. In its modern form, it presents nine personality patterns arranged in a diagram as points around a circle. Each number, or point, represents a root "addiction" which defines the shape of the personality.

I am, by nature, sceptical about such things, but what astonished me was the uncanny accuracy with which it described several people I know. My eye was drawn to the description of the Number Three personality, known as "The Performer". Number Threes are popular go-getters, leaders of teams. Their addiction is success, and they get things done. They project an attractive image, and have very sensitive antennae. They can walk into a room, sense the atmosphere immediately, and pitch their words perfectly.

The trouble with Threes, when they move to the unhealthy end of their personality spectrum, is that they can become deceitful. They are brilliant at reflecting back to their hearers what they want to hear in the first place. Threes adjust their convictions and language to suit the audience. Not only do they deceive others, but they deceive themselves. They are salesmen and women, selling themselves along with their product.

The more I studied, the more it dawned on me that I was reading a description of our prime minister. The Blessed Tony has the world at his feet.

It is too simple to see Blair as a Tory with attitude. Radical constitutional reform, a Freedom of Information Act, signing up to the Social Chapter and the introduction of a minimum wage are not your standard Conservative party meat-and-drink.

Yet Tony Blair confuses me. My unease deepened at the time of Diana's death. Blair has been lauded for saying the right things, for catching the mood of the nation. Let me make a personal minority confession: the prime minister's performance made me cringe, as did his theatrical reading at the funeral service. I glimpsed, I think, a ham actor at work.

It's too simple to say that he was insincere, but it is easy for self-deception to flow into a wider deception with which a needy public colludes. All that populist guff about "the people's princess" and the people's everything else, and all the warm-wordy feely-touchy pseudo-therapeutic language that goes with it, is simply blethers.

Like all extreme Threes on the Enneagramatical scale, Blair is a chameleon. He can change to suit the audience. He has the populist knack of sending an audience of disparate people away home believing that he has addressed their concerns. That ability was presumably effective in brokering the Northern Ireland deal.

Charisma, which the prime minister undoubtedly has, can easily move into mesmerising manipulation. Tony Blair is a telegenic salesman who believes in his product – even though that product changes from year to year. Look at him on the platform – the messianic eyes blazing with sincerity, the evangelical passion coming out of every pore. Trust me, is the message, and I will lead you to the promised land, where the lion will lie down with the lamb, where Rupert Murdoch will snuggle up with Tony Benn, and all things shall be well and all manner of things shall be well. Tony Blair is a cross between a world statesman and a double-glazing salesman, an intriguing mix of Bill Clinton and Billy Graham.

Private Eye has, as usual, got it right in its regular portrayal of the prime minister as a positive-thinking, feel-good, guitar-playing, happy-clappy vicar of St Albion's, with Peter Mandelson as churchwarden and Gordon Brown as parish treasurer.

Yet Blair has genuine reforming instincts and, as a good Number Three, he will deliver what he promises. He has it in him to become a great prime minister. That will only happen if he gets beyond image and makes genuinely tough decisions which risk turning friends into enemies. For instance, it is unrealistic to talk about justice for all without taking on the redistribution of wealth.

Blair needs people around him who will help him call his own inner bluff. The danger point for any Three comes when the successful image is confused with reality. If he inhales his own heady self-publicity then he risks losing his soul, even – and he will recognise the allusion – as he gains the whole world. Redemption for a Three, according to the Enneagram, comes when he or she breaks the image addiction, eschews fake emotion, and risks unpopularity.

Let's hear it for the Sufis. To understand the post-modern political scene, we maybe need a grip of medieval mystical psychology every bit as much as the apparently cool and rational, but actually voodoo-ridden, political pseudo-science.

A drop o' the Auld Kirk

Highland Park is a very good whisky. It has a very distinctive peaty flavour; I walk on the very peat moors which the Orkney distillery owns. It used to be the case early this century that a firkin of the amber fluid was delivered annually free of charge to the manse of St Magnus Cathedral.

In these days the incumbent was the legendary Dr John Rutherford. The whiskery cleric was known to imbibe the stuff with relish, before going off to visit the flock. And a right good minister he was, full of sage advice, full of the spirit.

He used to visit an old lady of the parish, who much appreciated the good doctor's ministrations. He would chat with her about this and that, then would read the scriptures, before concluding the visit with the "bonny words" (prayers). On one occasion, when he finished his prayers, the ancient crone asked him to pray again. He bowed over her again. Then she asked for more. He obliged. Then a third time, she asked for more bonny words.

While appreciating her piety and devotion, Dr Rutherford was curious. Why did she keep requesting more and more bonny words?

"It's yer braith, Dr Rutherford, it's yer braith," she replied in ecstasy.

She couldn't afford the stuff, and to inhale as the minister exhaled was the next best thing. Bonny words indeed.

Nowadays, she would sue for passive drinking.

Dr Rutherford used to go every Saturday to the barber's for a shave. Old Corsie liked a dram every bit as much as the meenister, and he had the tremors to prove it. Shaky hands on a swaying man carrying an open razor was not guaranteed to extend one's lifespan. You were safer at Sweeney Todd's.

One Saturday, the shoogly barber nicked the minister's face with his razor.

"Corsie, Corsie, it's the drink, it's the drink," remonstrated the cleric, more in sadness than in anger.

"Aye, Dr Rutherford," replied Old Corsie, "it maks the skin gey tender."

Game, set and match to Sweeney Corsie.

Sometimes people assume the Church of Scotland is against drink. It all depends which strand of the kirk you're dealing with. The Free Kirk tradition is Puritan in origin, though that aspect has softened. The broad Reformed tradition – known as the Auld Kirk – has never been against drink. In fact, to have a dram used to be called "taking a drop o' the Auld Kirk."

I've thought about all this in recent weeks. At the Christmas Eve service in St Magnus Cathedral, over 1,000 people lustily singing the carols produced an atmosphere that could have provided all the energy needed to light up Kirkwall for three days. The service could have been sponsored by Highland Park.

At this stage in January I've done more passive drinking than ever, as people have approached me. George MacLeod used to say of publicity that it was all right as long as you didn't inhale. I've inhaled sherry, whisky, gin, brandy, wine and Irn Bru in big quantities.

Passive drinking saves you an absolute fortune. You can end up in a coma free of charge. Is there a marketing niche here? Why haven't we Scots thought of this? Too busy engaging in active drinking, I suppose.

You can see the need for a knees-up in the bleak midwinter, especially in the dark, northern climes. At the end of January, Shetland has Up Helly a', the great fire festival which involves the burning of a Viking longship. Much fire water is consumed as well.

To get through a Scottish winter requires endurance. Whether it requires quite so much booze is another matter. "Don't mind me, I've had a wee refreshment," says the respectable elderly lady as she lurches forward.

I like the way matrons in middle class Glasgow say dinkily of their menfolk, "Oh, he likes a wee refresh!" That, roughly translated, meant ten pints in a session. The use of the diminutive is intended to give the illusion of a situation under control. A wee refresh! I've never met so many considerably over-refreshed men than in Glasgow.

January is furry-tongued payback time. It's also a time which has certain dangers. The drink which was such a sparkling gift in the festive season can quickly become a daily necessity to get through January. And February. And March.

January is also traditionally the season of remorse, as the financial and emotional bills for the festivities come flooding in. Along with them are fragmentary memories of parties in which you were sparkling and everyone else, of course, was unusually talkative and loud. "After four martinis, my husband turns into a disgusting beast," said one woman. "And after the fifth, I pass out altogether."

And there was the unmentionable behaviour of the normally inhibited office secretary, following in the footsteps of Dorothy Parker – "One more drink and I'll be under the host." Or there is the cringing remembrance of behaviour, summed up by the anonymous poet –

It was early last December,
As near as I remember,
I was walking down the street in tipsy pride;
No one was I disturbing
As I lay down on the curbing,
And a pig came up and lay down by my side.

As I lay there in the gutter
Thinking thoughts I shall not utter,
A lady passing by was heard to say:
'You can tell a man who boozes
by the company he chooses';
And the pig got up and slowly walked away.

All of this, unaccountably, makes me think of politics. Our lords and masters, refuelled at countless cocktail parties, will soon be breathing fire and brimstone back at Halitosis Hall itself, the great Westminster bear pit. There they will rail against mind-altering substances, before setting about the disabled.

Ach well. Only 350 passive drinking days till Christmas. Think what money you'll be saving. Cheers.

Three cheers for middle class guilt!

It is pandemonium. Crowds jostle and shout, people are selling things at the top of their voices, flower-bedecked pilgrims are kneeling before sacred shrines, a goat wails before being slaughtered. No, this is not Glasgow Cathedral on a Sunday morning: it is the fearsome Kalighat, the Hindu temple from which Calcutta gets its name.

The temple is dedicated to Kali, the consort of the God Shiva. According to legend, when Kali's corpse was cut up, one of her fingers fell there, since when it has been one of India's most important places of pilgrimage.

Kali, who is usually pictured with her raspberry-coloured tongue hanging out and carrying a bloodstained knife, is a goddess on whose side it is good to keep. She is not part of the Presbyterian pantheon (unless things have changed dramatically in the time I've been away). Kali represents the destructive side of the heavenly powers-that-be. She is an exciting, terrifying goddess, a powerful laxative from above.

As I make my way through the manic, jam-packed crowds, I am reminded of the terracing at Central Park, Cowdenbeath (only kidding). One of the temple priests leads us past the three-eyed Kali shrine. Each day, pilgrims bring a goat to be sacrificed, and once a year a water buffalo comes to a gory end. Then into the queue going round the fertility phallic lingam – Holy Willie's prayer! – and out to the water tank, where pilgrims purify themselves. It is a mixture of Old Testament sacrificial worship, circus, and street theatre.

What to make of it? This is as far away from douce Presbyterianism as it is possible to get. We've grown used to sanitised interpretations of sometimes scary ancient scriptures, *Sunday Post* mottos and IM Jollys with cheery wee Late Calls. The demanding, loving, and sometimes fearsomely unpredictable Jehovah of the Hebrew scriptures has been domesticated, tamed, reduced to the reasonable bloke-next-door – a decent and kindly, but dull and slightly deaf old buffer who tries to arrange things for the best.

That version may fit fairly comfortably in affluent and beneficent periods: even then, the blood seeps through from time to time. Tragedies and disasters bring jolting reminders that life is a very unpredictable and even capricious business. It Could Be You – for good or for ill. In India, life and death are very immediate. Life expectancy is low, abject poverty and intimations of death are highly visible.

Hinduism has sophisticated theologies, as any reading of the Upanishads will show. It has many scholarly and saintly devotees, and I have learned to respect its spirituality and learning. Much popular Hinduism is garish and grotesque, but it keeps alive an instinctive feel for the "left hand" of God, the dark side of the divine. India is a daily reminder of the mysterious, unjust, ravaging, ferocious aspects of life. The cult of Kali is irrational, crude and instinctive, but it corresponds to some dark realities which cannot be wished away.

Out into the mayhem outside, then right into the building next door – Mother Teresa's home for the dying. The work is legendary, of course, so that when people in the west hear the name Calcutta, they often speak the name of Mother Teresa. The notice-board informs us that there are 34 men and 22 women in the home today. Pavement dwellers who are seriously ill are brought in: they are cleaned up and cared for by nuns and volunteers from many countries.

Some people have criticised the western volunteers, accusing them of acting out of voyeurism, or middle class guilt. What I see impresses and moves me. I speak to one girl, from Herefordshire. She is dedicated and idealistic, and not in the least pretentious. Like the other volunteers, she is prepared to get her hands dirty – to wash the excrement-encrusted bodies of the derelict, abandoned, dying people, and hold their hands as they breathe their last.

Amid this decay and death, a sign is painted on the wall – *The Body of Christ. Whatever ye did to the least of these my brethren, ye did unto me.* These people, believers and half-believers, are living the doctrine, walking the walk. In scraping the shit off the wizened, hopeless bodies they are tending the body of the wounded Christ himself. If this be middle class guilt, then three cheers for middle class guilt! There is hope here in this place of dying, as well as idealism and compassion and, yes, heroism. One of the deficiences of our advanced twentieth-century west is that we have failed to provide the context and role models for genuine heroics. In this photo-opportunity world, we have become jaded, too cynical by half.

I step past the bodies in the streets outside. The poor do not hide themselves away conveniently. They are there – pressing in upon you – old before their time, deformed, blind, lame, fetid, repellent. You feel angry and impotent: angry that such poverty should exist at the end of the twentieth century, angry at the feelings it induces in you, angry because you have to push your way through the crowd to get to where you are going, angry at the political corruption, angry at your own complicity in poverty, enraged by your impotence in the situation.

I reflect on the proposal, reported recently in the Indian press, for a £10m Princess Diana theme park. Is this really the best we can do? And will the £760m Millennium dome simply reflect back to ourselves in a hall of mirrors the (substantial) material achievements of the west? Maybe the tumultuous shrine of Kali is nearer the human mark than the inglorious temple of Narcissus.

When sticking One's heid up the lum becomes a real drag

Prince Charles and I have something in common from our schooldays. No, HRH didn't go to school in Cowdenbeath too; for some inexplicable reason his parents sent him to Gordonstoun instead. What a mistake!

My parents decided not to send me to Gordonstoun because (a) they were a few thousand pounds short on the fees (b) they had never heard of the place, and (c) they wanted me to be part of a ruling elite. Beath High School – producer of such world leaders as Jim Baxter as well as my humble self – was, of course, a centre of imperial excellence.

What the Prince and I have in common is that we both smoked in the school lavvies. Now they're setting up a Europe-wide study of smoking in school kludgies and other such covert places. Will the research be conducted *in situ?* Will they use a lookout to watch for the heidie, or will the heidie be in there as well, having a surreptitious drag?

In my day, serious smokers served their apprenticeship in the lavvies. (That's why it's called peer pressure.) I started when I was 13. We actually began by smoking cinnamon sticks, then graduated to the real thing. Outside the toilets, some poor sucker was put on lookout to check for the neo-Nazi prefects, and we all puffed away and talked tough.

After a while, I graduated to stealing my mother's cigarettes. She smoked Senior Service. I can still remember the elegant white packs; indeed, as I write, I can re-experience the distinctive aroma of the pristine white cigarettes in the pack. When my mother was out, I would nick a fag, and smoke it up the chimney. (If my mum had come back early, I would have claimed I was looking for Santa Claus. Clever, eh?)

Now, there can be few things in life more stupid than sticking one's daft wee Cowdenbeath heid up a lum and puffing furiously at a cigarette, but there it is. ("How do you spend your leisure time?" "Actually, I stick my head up a chimney and smoke cigarettes." Oh. I see.) A hundred years or so earlier I would have been up a lum with a brush earning the odd bawbee from a cruel master; now I was half way up a sooty chimney, a debonair boy of the world, with a cigarette between my elegant fingers. Oh, the advance of civilisation! Oh, the evolutionary development of Homo Cowdenbeathius! (Did my pal Prince Charles nick fags from the Queen Mum and stick One's royal heid up the lum at Buckingham Palace? It's important that the royals know what the inside of a chimney looks like, that's what I say.)

I was brought up in a swirl of smoke. It's what made me the man I am. My chain-smoking dad gave up the fags at the age of 79. He was scared smoking would stunt his growth.

In teenage years, the important thing was to be able to talk and smoke at the same time. I could do all that and walk as well! That's what it means to be part of an elite. The fag would be put in the corner of the mouth, and you would drawl like the cowboys in the movies. Cool! The Lochgelly burdz went wild.

I finally gave up smoking at the age of 23. The moment of revelation came when I was sitting in the newsroom of the Edinburgh *Evening News* pounding away at an old Underwood typewriter. In the middle of the immortal words I was composing, I suddenly asked myself, "Have I just had a fag, or have I not?" It's the kind of question that the young Wittgenstein used to torment himself with. (We used to discuss the *Tractatus Logico-Philosophicus* while we smoked in the school lavvies in Cowdenbeath. Bet they didn't do that at muscular Gordonstoun – they were too knackered after running up and down mountains and having cold showers to stop them thinking about burdz.) Anyway, I couldn't answer the existential question, so I quit the habit there and then.

All this wasn't so long ago; but it now seems hard to remember that every room, every cinema, every restaurant you went into was full of smoke. You always went home smelling like an overdone finnan haddie. The one thing that was never mentioned was the word that dared not speak its name – cancer. The smoking habit wasn't just cool – it was slowly killing us.

Nowadays, like the heir to the throne – who is seeking to have the royal warrant taken away from Gallahers, the manufacturers of Senior Service – I hate to see so many youngsters smoking. The tobacco manufacturers are still literally making a killing. Kids are still as easily suckered, and people in Third World countries are being cynically targeted.

What do I do instead of smoking? Well, I've never been able to kick the habit of sticking my heid up lums. (I don't inhale, though.) Now, instead of smoking while in the chimney, I simply meditate on Wittgenstein's *Tractatus*. That's what the intellectual flower of Cowdenbeath do. Hey, I'll bet my smoke-free pal Prince Charles wishes every night that he'd gone to school in Cowdenbeath. He would have been free of eccentricity – like me – and much, much better equipped to rule the world.

This dark knight of the soul is dangerous

The *Sun* newspaper and its stablemate the *News of the World* thrive on the exposure of the sexual misdemeanours of the great and the not-so-good. In the pursuit of the details of bonking at the highest levels, these sainted investigators - doing their work of righteousness more in sorrow than in anger - labour on our behalf night and day, especially night. No drainpipe is too slippery to climb, no phone too difficult to bug, no bin bag too messy to empty.

In order to entrap a sportsman or media celebrity, disguise, deception and subterfuge are not disdained. No expense is spared in order to bring tidings and pictures of celebrities with their moral and physical breeks around their ankles. Thus are we informed and elevated. Were it not for the vigilance of these defenders of the nation's ethics, we might be totally unaware of these high-level couplings.

Strangely, though, the *Sun* and the *News of the World* unaccountably missed an unsavoury story about the activities of an international tycoon some time back. Mr Rupert Murdoch, aged 68, parted company with his second wife, Anna, after 32 years of marriage, and moved into a multi-million pound love nest with his 29-year-old Chinese lover, Wendy Deng. It's a pity the *Sun* and the *News of the Screws*, as the righteous paper is affectionately known in the trade, didn't know about it, otherwise they would have run 6-foot deep headlines like **Randy Rupe and Tasty Chinese Takeaway!** The *Sun* could have shown grainy pictures of the couple locked in sexual congress, taken through bedroom windows with a zoom lens. Reporters might have bugged the mansion and printed the breathless conversations verbatim, or retrieved passionate love notes from the rubbish bags. Seems they weren't up to the job this time around.

In fact, these two investigative journals must be slipping up, because they missed out on another scandal! A senior media man abandoned his wife and children to set up home with his lover, a wealthy international publisher. Silence from the *Sun* and the *News of the World*. They missed the opportunity for another juicy heading: **Love Rat Dumps Wife and Kids for Heiress!** Blew it again!

How did these two ever-vigilant tabloids contrive to miss both these scandals? The answer is very simple: both journals are owned by Mr Rupert Murdoch. And the lover in the second case was the daughter of the same Dirty Digger. Stones are left unturned, apparently, if it's the boss and his family who are transgressing. The zoom lenses are packed away. The rubbish bags remain unslit. Thus were we spared the usual pictures on pages 2,3, 4, 5 and 6; and also the great sermons about dirty deeds in high places, set among endless exclusive slavering picture-stories about people having sex with hamsters and such like.

A few years ago, Rupert Murdoch predicted that the time would come when there would only be three national dailies in Britain. He himself has used his vast resources to engage in a predatory, crippling price war. The fact that, say, the *Independent*, makes an important contribution to a healthy democracy is of no concern to Mr Murdoch. Making money is his business, and he takes no prisoners.

Not only does unflattering material about the nocturnal

activities of the saintly papal knight miraculously fail to appear in his own papers, he himself is conducting a moral crusade to keep Britain out of the European single currency. (What title shall we give him after getting his knighthood from the Pope? Lord Murdoch of Tits 'n' Bums? Answers, please, on a postcard). His newspaper editors apparently agree with him in every detail. They tell us in screaming headlines that we Britishers should not be taking lectures from Johnny Foreigner. Yet the man giving us this unbiased advice is an Australian who lives in the States and is a US citizen. So we are being told by a foreigner not to listen to foreigners. One does not need to have a strong sense of irony to see that this is a rather quixotic situation. It's also a dangerous situation. This international predator owns far too many chunks of the global print, television and film media. He has too much power for our own good.

The uncritical worship of the global market will eventually destroy those who are in its thrall, such as the leader of the Labour Party. What if Murdoch is right, and there will only be three national daily papers left in Britain in a few years? There is already a conspiracy of silence in the public prints about the activities of the main media players. For instance, the Barclay brothers who own the *Scotsman* are apparently going to bankroll the campaign against the single currency. What do we actually know about them?

Newspapers which zealously expose the frailties of politicians become very coy not only about their own ambiguous situations, but about other newspapers as well. Nelson, it seems, is alive and well and wearing a green eyeshade. Praise the Lord for *Private Eye,* and pass the ammunition.

Storm over Al Nino

There is, near Cambridge, a small and inoffensive village called Ugley. It has never bothered any other hamlet, has never tried to invade Kuwait or anything like that. Yet, it is giggled at, simply because of its name. The pressure eventually got to the members of the Ugley Women's Rural Institute, who decided to change their name. As a consequence, it is now officially known as 'The Women's Rural Institute (Ugley branch)'. No, I'm not making this up.

I thought about the Ugley women when I read about the campaign by Tony and Lorraine Holden to get the name of their street changed. It has been called, from time immemorial, Sluts Hole Lane. The road sign has been put outside their home, and they worry in case their two daughters may be affected. They would settle for Ugley Women's Lane any day.

Hey, but what about poor Al Nino from Nipomo, California? People are blaming him for the weather! They are, believe it or not, confusing the retired pilot with El Niño, the hurricane that has caused so much devastation. Angry people have been phoning Al, shouting at him, accusing him of responsibility for storms.

One man has even blamed Nino for the loss of his daughter's virginity, for heaven's sake! Apparently she couldn't go home one night because of storm damage caused by El Niño and her boyfriend had to take her in and.....well, this is a family column, and a veil must be drawn across the details.

Al Nino has never done anyone any harm in his life. Now, he can hardly leave his hoose for fear of attack by crazed Sunday School teachers and vicious Brown Owls whose trips have been ruined by a wee bit of wind (which is what feart people south of Orkney call a gale.)

And did you hear about Fred Widebottom? He got so fed up with jokes about his name that he changed it by deed poll. So now he answers to Kevin Widebottom. (Okay, I made that one up, but the others are absolutely true.)

Parents who inflict excruciating names on their children - such as Eileen Dover - should be hauled out and crucified in front of day-time confessional TV audiences. Imagine being named after the whole promotion-wining Cowdenbeath team of 1924! I'll never forgive you, dad.

Names can be empowering, or downright embarrassing. What if you have a sensible name, but people call you 'duck'? Well, it seems that the ducks and hens are fighting back. According to a survey by *Bella* magazine - "Haw Bella, is that you hen?"- almost half of those who replied said that they objected to being called 'dear'. Probably even more to being called cheap.

Staff from a number of institutions have been instructed not to use pet names. Trying to tell people in Glasgow to stop calling girls 'hen' would be about as productive as trying to prise the Lord Provost's chain off Pat Lally. (Women, though, seem to have stopped calling me 'son' over the last year or two. I'm sure it's just politeness.)

Incongruous names can cause amusement. As part of a general knowledge quiz, I once asked some youngsters to give me the name of an Old Testament prophet beginning with the letter "I".

"Ian," replied one lad, cheerfully.

"Let us now read some verses from the prophet Ian." Doesn't quite have the same ring as Isaiah.

Supposing the author of the fourth gospel had been called 'Jock'. The Prologue from Jock's Gospel: lacks a certain *je ne sais quoi.*

Would the history of Christianity be different if the disciples had all been public school heroes with names like Nigel, Torcuil and 'Bunny'?

"And Jesus saith unto him, 'Nigel, be a good chap would you, and take up thy cross and follow me...." Maybe not.

Or again, how about: "And Erchie, Boab and Senga ran to the empty tomb....." No? Actually, if that had been their names - not common names in first century Palestine, admittedly - they would now be Saint Erchie, Saint Boab and Saint Senga, and their bright wee faces would be looking radiantly out of stained glass windows all over Europe.

This inspirational meditation on the significance of names takes me on to titles. Thanks to all those who suggested titles for Rupert Murdoch, wacky papal knight. Not a single one of them is printable in this family column.

One 'friend' phoned to ask if I had heard the news that the *Herald* had just been taken over by Mr Murdoch, who was heading for Scotland with his aides. I had already mentally cleared my desk, withdrawn the savings I had been hoarding to buy a papal knighthood, and set out for a secret hideaway at Skara Brae, before he confessed that it was all a joke. A joke! I put on ten years in a minute. Even fewer women will call me 'son' now.

I now have a secret strategy should that dreadful event take place. I will change my name and my appearance, and keep on writing the column! Never fear! Grieve not! I shall grow a beard (try it now, please, with a black felt pen on my gentle and kindly features.) The Dirty Digger will never ken it's me!

The name beside the strangely familiar bearded face will be Al Nino (In new *Sun-Herald* speak, "The Man who Writes a Storm!" Geddit?) And if you want to send me more Murdoch insults, my new address will be Sluts Hole Lane (e-mail: sluts@papalknight.co.uk) The resistance campaign headquarters will be the underground bunker of the Women's Rural Institute (Ugley branch).

Ugley ladies, call me 'son' and I'm yours! Salman Rushdie, eat your heart out! Free the Ugley One!

Where there's a Will, there's a way out

A couple, both in their nineties, went to their lawyer to ask about a divorce. When asked why they were separating after all these years, they replied, "We wanted to wait until the children were dead."

That black-humoured story came to mind while reflecting on the plight of Will Carling. The tale of England's former rugby captain is a postmodern parable which has everything in it – celebrity, sport, sex, greed, spin-doctoring, glamour, psychobabble and a book-launch. Oh yes, and a shadowy show-biz relationship with Diana, Princess of Wales. This Carling Special has got something for everyone. Except, perhaps, a little baby boy called Henry. More of that later.

The first thing to be said about Will Carling is that he is a good rugby player. His fortune has been to be captain of England at a time when sport, television, sponsorship, hype and money have come together to spectacular effect.

As a prominent sportsman, Mr Carling was lionised by the media. Business also quickly saw the potential of the on-field captain, and he was soon involved in sponsorship and advertising deals. He was also invited to speak at expensive leadership seminars which, by all accounts, consisted of the recital of the most vacuous of New Age mantras. His marriage to the glamorous Julia, model and television presenter, increased his celebrity rating.

Enter, flirtatiously on left, a golden princess. She makes doe-eyes at our handsome hero, who is up for the game, as they say nowadays. Diana observes, "I think you are unhappy, are you not?" Will is flattered by intimate conversation with the most-photographed woman in the world; the sad princess is pleased by the attention of such a good-looking celebrity.

The news of the series of emotional rucks is – inevitably – leaked, but by whom? The parties express outrage; but both, as devotees of the Temple of Narcissus, are not entirely displeased by the headlines. The tabloids think it is Christmas; the beautiful Julia spits nails, which will eventually be hammered into the coffin of their marriage.

The soap opera is not over. Will settles down with another model, Ali Cockayne, and declares himself to be in love. They are the picture of happiness; until, that is, Ali gives birth to their child. Will confides to whoever will listen that he is finding it hard to cope with the fact that Ali's attention is divided. Will is Unhappy again, and when Will is Unhappy, someone has to pay the price. When his son is 11 months old, Will drops the bombshell that he is leaving to set up home with the understanding wife of a friend. Bye, bye, Ali and little Henry.

The news is leaked – just at the time when Will's autobiography is due to be serialised in a tabloid newspaper. As George MacLeod was wont to say, "If you think that is a coincidence, I wish you a very dull life." The pictures of Will and his new love are on the front page of most papers, and the book is in demand in the shops. Will's agent is pleased.

Mr Carling is bewildered by the fact that not everyone is congratulating him on his recent key life-changes. Asked whether he regrets the decision to walk out on his partner and son, he tells The *Herald*, “I didn’t believe I should stay in a relationship for the sake of a child. I don’t think that is what life’s all about.”

Eh? Would you run that one by us again, Will?

It is probably not productive to press Will for his verdict on what life is all about. The views of a wealthy 32-year-old manchild on the meaning of life may lack a certain rigour. What would be more instructive would be to sit at the feet of young Henry Carling as he grows up in a hard emotional world; or to talk to a 32-year-old woman who struggles to bring up her family as her partner goes off to find himself.

What is depressing is that Henry’s other name could be Legion. There are so, so many. Figures released last week show that Britain currently has the highest separation and divorce rate in Europe. The emotional and financial costs can hardly be measured.

This article is not a plea to go back to the “good old days” when people stayed in relationships which were miserable, and often abusive. What is clear, though, is that we are producing an emotional holocaust in which children are the innocent victims. The nurture and upbringing of children is a demanding vocation which is not honoured or supported properly in our society. There are times when it is right for people to part, especially when the pain of their staying together is too much for the children to bear. But a culture in which divorce is not the last resort but a much earlier one, is a culture which is seriously injurious to children. It affects all classes of society. The chairman of the Headmaster’s Conference said only this week that family breakdown is the primary problem in independent schools, presenting a much greater threat to pupils’ well-being than alcohol or drugs.

When children are on the scene, the equation changes dramatically. They take priority. They didn't ask to be born, and they should not be wounded or abandoned. When Mr Carling says, "I didn't believe I should stay in a relationship for the sake of a child", he is saying something irreducibly grievous. He is wrong.

To stay for the sake of a child is an honourable human commitment. If "finding oneself" can only be achieved at the cost of the emotional security of vulnerable little ones, then serious questions have to be asked.

Where there is a Will, apparently, there is a way out. But not for Henry. If there is no point at which individualism reaches its limits, then we become that most terrible thing – a society in which our children are only to be pitied.

"Donnie" Dewar, statesman with attitude

Imagine it if you will: Donald Dewar as the subject of an image makeover. Yesterday's news that he is to have his own spin doctor is only the beginning. A thousand careers will be launched on the back of a successful transformation. The Secretary of State for Scotland represents the ultimate re-packaging challenge.

First, a "colour consultant" decides that Mr Dewar is a "Spring" person. He should wear pastel shades. It is decreed that some – but not too much – new hair will be transplanted, and the stylist suggests that the Scottish Secretary part his new strands somewhere about his oxter. When out and about the streets he will wear a baseball hat, turned back-to-front. In Glasgow, he will wear a crash helmet.

The specs are a problem – too big, make him look too much like a malnourished Biggles. Eventually, it's decided that he will have contact lenses – they will give him a steely look on television. The face is no adman's dream. He is booked in for plastic surgery at a London clinic. New Labour, new face. ("Mr Mandelson will be doing his ward rounds in a minute, sir.") He is also to have silicone implants in his shoulders. Sexy.

Cool gear: a leather jacket, Oasis tee-shirt, jeans and

boots for casual appearances; a dark, sharp, authoritative double-breasted Alex Salmond suit for when he has to outsmart everyone else. Full Highland dress for when the Nats are doing well in the polls. The rest of his wardrobe will be incinerated in the public interest.

Speech: definitely a problem. Fitted with a device which sends an electrical shock through the system with every “um”. It is agreed that he will be taught how to walk by an actor. Sean Connery’s name is suggested, but curtly rejected. From now on, he will be “Donnie” Dewar, the Statesman with Attitude. Ready when you are, for the re-launch of the Secretary of State.

It’s open season on Donald Dewar. For the last few weeks there has been a stream of stories about his political troubles, and how he urgently needs a new image and a team of spin doctors. He can do no right, it seems, from decision-making to speaking to walking.

This column presents the case for the defence. In fact, today we launch the Save The Donald campaign, seeking to preserve this endangered political animal. This mighty column, which belongs to and supports no party, is dedicated to conserving not only the whale, the bison and the Lochgelly bumblebee, but national treasures like Mr Dewar. We want to save him from the image-makers and the spinners, and preserve him for the nation as he is.

Why do we like Mr Dewar? Because he is the genuine article, that’s why. He’s the political equivalent of real ale. He is an outstanding Scotsman, who is making Scotland a better place.

I couldn’t care less that he lopes, stammers, and has a 1950s East European dress sense. He has genuine compassion for the underdog. The ultimate delivery of a powerful Scottish parliament was achieved with an inspiring, stunning virtuoso performance. He is a class act.

It is interesting that in the midst of all his recent woes,

people having been willing him out of his troubles. Of how many people in political life could that be truthfully said? It's because he is a national leader with fundamentally decent instincts. Okay, he may look and move like a misanthropic 18th century Presbyterian divine with haemorrhoids, and may appear as much fun as Ebeneezer Scrooge at Happy Hour. But he is actually a witty, humane and entertaining character, a political addict who actually believes that there is more to life than politics.

Donald Dewar is a politician with a hinterland, a civilised man of literature and life who must be kept out of the hands of the glitzy packagers at all costs. I much prefer him and his ilk to the on-message speaking-clocks who are increasingly dominating our political life. The ghastly spin doctors are the curse of our modern age, drip-dripping stories into the ears of lazy journalists.

Someone like Dewar will have good times and bad times. The fight between Edinburgh and Glasgow for the fledgling parliament was always going to leave bruised egos, whatever the decision. There are occasions when the normally courteous and gentlemanly Secretary of State cannot resist the temptation to suddenly stick the political heid on someone, but the balance comes down in his favour. He is glaikit, he is brilliant, and he is ours.

Here is the good news. Donald Dewar cannot be made-over. That is a virtue, not a failing. I hope he resists the image manipulators – those wonderful savants who gave us, for instance, the toe-curling pictures of Michael Forsyth, George Robertson, et al Saving Scotland from Drugs while wearing ridiculous baseball hats the wrong way round on their demented wee Scottish heids. Imagine calling that frightening glimpse of bedlam a "photo opportunity"!

And do you remember Billy "Mad Dog" Hague – with yet another mandatory baseball hat – looking like a wizened, slow-witted five-year old? The bunnet actually looked worse than the original Baby Dome it was intended to conceal. Believe it or not, that preposterous picture was dreamed up by an image consultant on a fat salary. These are the kind of people they want to let loose on oor Donald.

No, don't submit, Donald. Keep up the Ministry of Silly Walks. This column is campaigning for you to be declared a Listing Person by Historic Scotland. You should be pronounced a national monument and have a conservation order slapped upon you (subject to planning permission from the Secretary of State for Scotland, of course.) If the critics and image-consultants are getting to you, tell them to get, um, stuffed; then rise up and be an abomination again.

New image for the Secretary of State? I'm with you at the barricades, Donald. We shall overcome. The fightback starts here.

An open letter to Cardinal Thomas Winning

Dear Tom – I have stood at the ecumenical barricades with you. Like you and with you, I have endured verbal tongue-lashings from Pastor Jack Glass. I have had venomous letters for allowing a requiem mass for George Mackay Brown in St Magnus Cathedral.

In short, I have fought in more than a few ecumenical campaigns, and have the scars to prove it. So when I unbite my tongue in response your latest observations on the ecumenical movement, it goes without saying that I do so with a sense of respect, and affection, for yourself. But something cries out to be said.

In your recent article in the *Herald*, you aver that the movement towards Christian unity is threatened by the ordination of women, and also by the churches' radically different approaches to moral issues. You cite specifically contraception, abortion, and divorce.

I detect the faint sound of a song behind the words of this deeply discouraging piece. That song is "The Cry is No Surrender". I suspect that your article will play well in Rome. What is depressing is that it will also be seen as confirming the worst head-shaking prophecies of the Rev Ian Paisley and his ilk.

When I talk to other Catholics in Scotland, including priests, I get a different story, a gentler song, a more generous set of longings and affirmations.

But are things as clear-cut as your article implies?

Take divorce. Not allowed. What take its place, though, is annulment – a procedure which looks a bit like, er, divorce (and remarriage in church) for people who are not permitted to believe in divorce. Traditionally, it has favoured the rich and the powerful. What this produces among ordinary people is not clarity but cynicism.

Birth control. Not allowed. At least, by means of a pill (unnatural). It is allowed, though, by means of a thermometer (unnatural). Your Grace knows full well that many, many Catholics have long since departed from the official teaching – not out of hedonism or rebelliousness, but because they find the Church's teaching confusing and contradictory. If so many lay people and priests openly depart from the official line, is it not implausible to talk as if there were a great gulf between Catholics and Protestants?

Clerical marriage. Not allowed. But if you are a married priest fleeing the Anglican Church because of your opposition to women, then, yes, you can be ordained a priest of the Roman Catholic Church.

Abortion. I admire the Catholic Church's unfashionable confronting of the issue in the face of unpopularity. But all churches are opposed in principle to abortion, and only regard it as morally permissible in very restricted circumstances. If, for instance, an 11-year-old girl in Bosnia who had been gang-raped by soldiers and had turned to the Cardinals for guidance, what would they say to her? To talk of moral absolutes is one thing; to deal compassionately and pastorally in that kind of situation is agonisingly difficult, as any priest or minister knows.

Ordination of women. Not allowed. For the moment.

Is the Roman Catholic Church really going to maintain until the end of time that those women who have felt a call to the priesthood have simply misheard – that the message was actually intended for the men standing beside them? This is not a matter of feminism or political correctness. Will the growing movement for women's ordination within the Catholic Church face blanket opposition from the hierarchy forever?

Inter-communion. Not allowed. Unless, that is, you happen to live in certain parts of Europe, or Africa, or America. You state unequivocally that inter-communion is not a present possibility. What is missing is the acknowledgement not only of the pain which is inflicted by this ruling, but of the damaging public statement made by Christians sitting back-to-back at the communion table, while preaching reconciliation.

As a Protestant who has enormous respect for the spirituality and worship of the Roman Catholic Church, my experience and observation tell me that there is tremendous commitment, generosity and faith among Catholics in Scotland. Yet conscientious Catholics who raise the kind of issues I have been talking about are so often made to feel disloyal. It gives me no happiness to say it, but the Roman Catholic Church in Scotland conveys the impression of a lack of transparency and openness.

Why is this defensiveness necessary? Are the faithful simply to be telt, and remain telt? That might have been good enough 100 years ago, but I suspect that you are trying to contain a revolution of the spirit which is ultimately uncontainable.

You rightly point out that ecumenical relationships in Scotland are much improved. Perhaps, though, we are in danger of wallowing in euphoria simply because Protestants and Catholics no longer gouge out each others' eyes over theological minutiae. The Christian churches should perhaps celebrate the Millennium by apologising to Scotland for the damage we have caused. We should certainly refrain from lecturing everyone about reconciliation.

Our churches are prisoners of their own histories. I'm not remotely suggesting that we Proddies have got it right. But instead of assigning non-negotiable status to positions which are often matters of historical accident, we should be seeking ways of getting each other out of jail. If we can do that, tremendous energies will be released.

If we start from the assumption that nothing can change, our prophecies will be fulfilled. Can we not come out from behind our barricades and images and public posturing and rejoice in what unites us, as well as dealing truthfully with what divides us? Can we move into an exciting time of celebration, repentance and wide-ranging dialogue about the things that really matter?

Your Grace, I believe that a clear choice lies before you.

I believe that you, Thomas Winning, now need to decide whether to settle for being a defensive tribal chief: or to trust your less cautious and more generous instincts and become the genuinely visionary leader that the Scottish churches need as we stand on the brink of a new Millennium.

Embarrassing truth about Cowdenbeath's ugliest son

So now we ken. Tony Blair's most embarrassing moment, as told to a 13-year old interviewer on BBC's Newsround, came when he was visiting President Clinton in the White House. The prime minister looked down and realised "with horror" that his socks were hanging round his ankles. Golly Gosh! I knew this guy was too good to be true. If this truly is his most excruciating moment, he has not lived too dangerously. Not like his friend at the White House, Buffalo Bill himself, who has been caught in the Oval Office with more than his socks around his ankles.

Surely Tone – as I call him when I speak to him regularly – has had more embarrassing moments than that? After all, he works with John Prescott. And when the Iron Laddie was publicly compared with Mrs Thatcher, was that not more cheek-reddening than having his socks round his daft wee ankles?

Almost all of my life so far has been embarrassing. It started when I was born. The doctor pronounced that I was the ugliest baby he had ever seen. Not only that, he said to my mother, pointing at me, "Know what I'd do with him?" As he uttered these kindly words, he pulled down on an imaginary toilet chain. Gee, I do love that doctor's sense of humour!

Now, friends, let me tell you this: to be the ugliest baby in Cowdenbeath – even uglier than Dennis Canavan – is not the greatest start in life. So things started badly and fell away, as they say in Glasgow. One day, as a schoolboy, I saw a pal of mine in the distance. I decided to play a merry jape on him. I would steal up on him quietly, and suddenly jump on his back! It's actually quite hard to run 500 yards silently – try it now, if you please – but us Renaissance Men from Cowdenbeath can handle the pressure. Anyway, my friend never knew what hit him till I landed on him. Gotcha!

There was only one problem. It wasn't my friend at all. It was a complete stranger. I was so traumatised that I remained perched on his shoulders. What does one say in such a situation? "It's a bit drizzly today, isn't it?" Or talk about the view? "It's marvellous. You can even see the coal bings of Lochgelly from up here!" The spell was broken when the innocent victim, his charmless face turned up towards this numpty on his back, asked bluntly and directly, "Who the f*** are you?" (I've been wrestling with that existential question ever since. Kierkegaard had a lot to say about it. But that's another story altogether.)

As a journalist, I had lots of embarrassing moments. Surely, though, the sequence would change when I became a divinity student? After all, God was now on my side! I and another student were asked to take a service in Danderhall. Precisely what the good people of Danderhall had done to deserve us I cannot remember. Anyway, the service had a memorable beginning. There was a wee procession down the aisle, in which the Bible-bearing beadle was followed by my good self, followed by my friend. Unfortunately, I got too close to the beadle, and caught the heel of his shoe, which half came off. Then, in what must be a statistical freak, my pal caught my heel.

What was intended as a dignified Presbyterian procession turned into a hobbling Monty Python farce. The congregation sobbed with laughter.

Onward and downward. When I was a meenister in Easterhouse, it was my turn to go to the General Assembly of the Kirk. Because it was also Christian Aid Week, I could only go through on the Wednesday, at about lunch time. It was a glorious summer day, and I was totally knackered. (Doing relentless Good Works fair takes it oot ye.) As I emerged, blinking, from Waverley station, the Assembly was skailing. With all these people in black suits and dog collars, it looked like an undertakers' convention. It took me a nano-second to decide. I would spend the afternoon in Princes Street Gardens, like Jonah, asleep! The gardens were packed. I got the last deck chair, and went down to the front of the crowd.

What a disaster! I simply couldn't put the deck chair up. I tried it this way and that, and, getting more and more tense as the sniggers grew louder, I ended up with my crazed Fife heid sticking through the damned thing! The Calvinist God's revenge! What to do? Enter on left the omnipresent rescuing wee wifie. Glaring at the crowd, the compassionate woman set the deck chair right way up in one swift movement, and I sank into it, face like beetroot.

These are only a few of the printable embarrassing episodes. Why am I telling you all this stuff? Firstly, because I've got a column to fill. Secondly, because I'm an unreconstructed Presbyterian masochist. Tone, I'll take your twee socks around the ankles any day. And when you're at it, pal, get a life.

Real victim is in his tiny grave

Two pictures haunt the mind this week. First, the look of relief on the face of English au pair Louise Woodward in a Boston courtroom as judge Hiller Zobel announces her freedom. Second the tortured grimace of Scottish paedophile Steven Leisk as he is led out of Aberdeen High court to begin a 25-year jail sentence.

Then two contrasting scenes. In the Rigger pub in Elton, Louise Woodward's home village, people cheer and cry and laugh and hug one another. The banners "Louise is innocent" fly. Outside the High court in Aberdeen, a baying mob cries "scum" and "animal" as Leisk is led away.

Woodward is known to the world simply as "Louise". Leisk is referred to as a "monster". Yet what links these two people is this: after due process of law, they have both been declared responsible, in some form or another, for the death of a child.

The two cases are totally different, of course, but they raise issues about instant judgement by emotion, the power of television, and how we value our children.

The post-Diana mood in Britain is a strange one. It is as if there is a restless, gathered sense of emotion searching for a collective focus, any focus. Louise Woodward as icon? The notion is grotesque. The *Sun* newspaper, in full, nauseating, populist mode, called her – seriously – "the light of our lives". This way lies madness.

As the Massachusetts court opera soap opera developed, Louise Woodward became the frightened victim, set up by evil forces. She became the fragrant English girl scapegoated by twisted, brash American justice. As the public emotional head of steam developed, television came into its own, feeding the frenzy. Cameras were in the Rigger pub, of course. Wonder why the vicar was always in the front of the crowd? Because the television director placed him there, that's why.

People who saw and heard only a fragment of the evidence moved to instant judgement. They just knew; they didn't need to trouble with such a distracting thing as evidence. Not only was Louise completely innocent, it was the parents who were guilty. Either the father did it, or the mother. The instant judges just knew by the look of the parents, who didn't show enough emotion, weep enough.

Television is a deceptive and sometimes destructive medium. It selects and distorts, while presenting the image of objectivity. Yes, the camera can lie.

When Louise was found guilty, after the failure of her theatrical defence team's high-risk strategy, the conspiracy theories took wings. The Internet became the place where grievers and grievance-merchants met. Money poured in to the "Free Louise" fund. Newspapers ran phone-ins. The au pair looked lonely and frightened. Goodbye England's Rose? The bizarre mythology doesn't bear thinking about. Justice does not come by way of phone-ins, slogans or opinion polls, but by compassionate and careful weighing up of evidence.

The much maligned American justice system delivered a verdict which was humane and – so far as one can ever understand these things – fair. The confused and sad Louise Woodward, will eventually come home but not, please God, as a heroine.

In the meantime, the real victim of the tragedy, Matthew Eappen, is in his tiny grave. He will not grow old, as we that are left.....

In Aberdeen, there is no sympathy for Steven Leisk as he starts a life sentence. His deeds have been truly vile, and he must be kept away from children for life. Yet a searchlight on his life reveals a pathetic character. Brutally abused himself as a child, he was traumatised by his work as a medical orderly in the army in the Falklands, clearing up dismembered bodies. He will now be repeatedly attacked by prisoners until, perhaps, he breaks and commits suicide. There will be few tears shed for him, on television or elsewhere.

The understandable demonising and hounding of paedophiles masks the fact that most child abuse happens in the home, committed by trusted relatives: or, as we see time after time, in public institutions registered for the care for children. The public humiliation of known offenders conceals the simple fact that if every "monster" and every slightly dodgy au pair in the world were strung up, the mass of child abuse would still be left undealt with.

There are further disturbing questions about other ways in which children are abused emotionally. Why are kids regularly handed over to untrained people all day and every day? Why is the care of young children one of the most undervalued professions? Why is it so often essential in a two-parent family that both parents work full-time? If it is essential for economic survival reasons, why are so many jobs paid so poorly? If it is not for economic survival, what values and expectations underlie these decisions? What support is there for single parents struggling to bring up kids? What has happened to the dream of a society where both parents can work part-time and share in the upbringing of the children? What has happened to the notion of worksharing? Why is it that

Britain has the longest working-hours in Europe, meaning that parents are exhausted by the time they get home, with little left over for the children?

All these issues affect children very deeply. So too does the emotional holocost of family break-up and divorce. There are times when divorce is the only compassionate last resort, but the emotional, psychological and economic costs of a 60 per cent divorce rate are overwhelmingly damaging for children's lives. A culture in which abortion plays such a prominent part is hardly a child-friendly culture either.

These are complex and difficult and uncomfortable questions, and it is easier to mount a campaign to rescue a au pair or hound a "monster" than it is to address them with honesty and determination. Despite all the public sentimentality, we are not producing a society which nurtures and cares for children. Is there any emotion to spare?

Donald, whaur's yer broon troosers?

Oh dear, oh dear, oh dear. How many times can a human being hear the kindly and shining Dougie Donnelly say, "And that's our World Cup dream over again" without foaming at the mouth? Once more, dear auld Scotia is not happy bunny land. As graduates of the Scottish School of Disappointment Studies, we should forgo the usual national orgy of recrimination, and stop confusing the end of the World Cup with the end of the world.

It's time to look, as Monty Python would insist, on the bright side of life. One slight personal compensation is not having to listen to *Flower of Scotland* for a wee while. When I suggested in a throwaway remark a couple of weeks ago that the cringe-making song was a less than adequate anthem for the nation, some people reacted as if I had just assaulted their defenceless granny. Well, I'm donning the flak jacket again, ready for more punishment. Like Colin Hendry, this noble and public-spirited column is prepared to stick its heid in a tumble drier if there is a ball to be won.

Flower of Scotland is a pleasant – if baleful – ditty but, as a national anthem, it simply can't take the strain. Sung once or twice it's OK, but after several renditions it rots the brain. It is too close for comfort to the “Hoots mon!” school of Scottish singing, of which Andy Stewart, of blessed memory, was the great exemplar.

Remember the White Heather Club? “Come in, come in, it’s fine tae see ye. How’s yersel? Yer lookin’ grand.” What is required is a kilt, shoulders that go up and down, and a nasal twang. It is a very distinctive sound. To carry it off, all you need to do is throw in a few words like “heilan”, “hame”, “glen”, “granny”, “purple” and “heather”. Some military references never go amiss, particularly about battles against the English long ago.

I invite you try it now, to experience the effect. Please put down your *Herald,* stand up, make your shoulders go up and down, sing through your hooter to any vaguely Scottish tune, and moan something inarticulate about your auld granny and her hame.

If you’re in a railway compartment, why not try walking up and down the passage-way as you sing? The commuters will love it, will even join in (though try not to collide with another *Herald* reader who’s doing the same thing.) For an encore, give them “There was a soldier, a Scottish soldier”, with arm-swinging and marching actions. If you’re at home, you may not frighten the English, but you will terrify your dug. Go on, give it a whirl! You have nothing to lose but your brains....

Well, I’m sure you feel cheered up after doing that, because it’s fun, so it is. You see, you can only do the business tongue in cheek. The problem arises when you take your tongue out of your cheek and turn this kind of sentimental drivel into something approximating to a national anthem.

Most of us Scots didn’t have grannies in heilan hames. They might have been in old folk’s hames, but not necessarily in the Highlands. My own granny lived in Old Cumnock in Ayrshire, until the family moved up in the world and flitted to Cowdenbeath. She only ever saw hills and glens on shortbread tins; what she saw out of her window was unromantic pit bings.

But back to *Flower of Scotland.* Take Murrayfield, the home of Scottish rugby, where the song took off as an anthem. Isn't there something inherently preposterous about 60,000 chartered accountants and civil servants in blazers bawling about sending proud Edward's army homeward tae think again? Let's face it: the bulk of the crowd, if they were handed a claymore and told to repel even a fraction of Edward's army, would be frozen to the spot. Donald, whaur's yer broon troosers?

And what about Princess Anne trilling away about sending the English king back to base? Doesn't it bring a lump to your wee Scottish throat? No, actually, no and no again. Give us a break.

One of the enduring television images of the World Cup was of that civilised and peaceable man, Craig Brown, feeling compelled to mouth words before the cameras about hills being bare and standing up against proud Edward's bloody army yet again. Have we had a national sense of humour by-pass? The whole thing is too ridiculous for words.

Yet no politician would dare speak against *Flower of Scotland.* There are too many votes to be lost, too many populist tabloids baying for blood. Singing the toe-curling anthem has become a Scottish political virility test.

Why are we so obsessed about re-fighting Bannockburn, or, after a few pints, shedding some maudlin, vicarious tears over corpse-strewn Culloden? If we have to sing about battles, then I'm proud of my mother and father's generation for standing shoulder to shoulder with their English, Welsh, and Northern Irish brothers and sisters against proud Adolf's airforce in Britain's darkest hour, in the face of the Nazi racist menace. I'd like to celebrate their courage and decency, but I don't want to turn it into a national anthem either.

Scotland is a country with wonderful wordsmiths, songwriters and composers. Can't we produce a national song that doesn't have us perpetually covered in woad and wading up to our oxters in blood and heather, seeking out, or fleeing from, the English? Even in Highland Scotland, the punters had more to fear from fickle and treacherous Scottish clan chiefs than from English warlords.

Now, I am battening down the Orcadian hatches, going underground till the slings and arrows are over. I've got a telly, and some pies and bovril, garnered in foolish anticipation of Scotland reaching the next round. Oh mince of Scotland, when will we see yer pies again?

Ach, well. There's always the next World Cup. And, hopefully, a new song to sing.

Stars of the mobile circus

What became of all the clippies who used to man, or woman, the buses in Glasgow? Did they become social workers, or stress counsellors, or comediennes? More likely, they simply ended up on the dole.

I thought about that this week when I was down at the headquarters of the great British Broadcasting Company to record some stuff for a breathlessly expectant nation, and to visit the *Herald* office, this mighty column's Mission Control. As a dreamy guy who now lives in a place with no traffic lights and only two roundabouts – when the first one was put in place, Radio Orkney had to explain to motorists how to use a roundabout, as everyone kept politely waiting for the others to move, then they all moved at the same time – I had several near-death experiences simply trying to cross the busy Glasgow streets.

It was when I went to get on a bus that I thought about the clippies, and indeed about John Prescott. The jowly Transport minister has never looked convincing to me wobbling on a bike or hanging on to an Underground strap for all these risible "photo-opportunities" – he's basically a Jaguar man – but he keeps telling us to use public transport.

Who am I to refuse to obey the Deputy Prime Minister of Great Britain? So here I am, standing obediently at a

Glasgow bus stop, and that's when my problems begin. (I bet you thought this Great Column always travelled in the back seat of a chauffeur-driven Mercedes. As a *Herald* writer, naturally, that's how I usually travel; but like John Prescott, I like to do my "Man of the People" bit now and again and mingle with the vulgar throng.)

Anyway, the notice at the bus shelter says that you have to have the right fare, and that the driver doesn't give any change. Fine, except that, as a Great Columnist, I don't carry anything as small as coins. I don't deal in bawbees; and my staff carry my wallet.

So what will the fare be? Well, the notice doesn't tell you. I tell you, this system must have been designed by sadists who wanted to torment foreign tourists and dozy punters from the isles. You must have the right fare – but we won't tell you what the right fare is! Ha! Gotcha! You won't come back to Glasgow in a hurry, pal! Might as well stick the heid on you at the same time, to teach you a lesson!

There's a queue to get on. It takes for ever, as the grumpy driver explains to bewildered Japanese visitors the nature of the system which is ripping them off. The bus then lurches off, through the heavy traffic, until the next stop, when the same pantomime begins all over again. Because the driver is the one dealing with all the fares and the complaints as well as driving the wretched vehicle, it is a slow and frustrating process.

That's the point at which I thought of the clippies, with great nostalgia. Do you remember the days when the driver's job was to drive the bus, and the bus conductress collected the fares, dealt with complaints, and kept everybody entertained? You got fast service, efficiency and vaudeville all in one journey. It was great value, and it wasn't all that long ago. I'm glad that they tell me it's progress, otherwise I wouldn't have kent.

The world of the clippie was a complete culture in its own right. As a fresh-faced young Proddy cleric with three-foot deep dog collar, I would proffer the fare – they gave change in those days – and the kindly woman would invariably walk past my outstretched hand saying deferentially, "That's all right, Father." I would spend the rest of the journey alternately thanking God for the Roman Catholic Church, and sweating in case an inspector came on.

Some of the clippies had a great way with words. One day, a dog got on and went upstairs. The conductress ran up the stairs shouting, "Is this ony o' youse dug?" The rest of the journey was spent pondering the wondrously economical syntax.

Clippies were never lost for words. On one occasion a perspiring man struggled on to a crowded bus with a double bass. It was a terrific squeeze, but he just managed it. The conductress fixed him with a quizzical look and said, "Ah hope that when ye get there, son, they ask ye tae play." No wonder English comedians died with their boots on at the Glasgow Palladium.

I wonder: did they interview clippies, or did they simply audition them? Not only were they actresses; they were singers, counsellors and bouncers as well. The buses were centres of conviviality on wheels. Each bus was a piece of moving theatre. A good clippie would encourage the passengers to contribute to the soiree. You got passengers who would address the whole bus on the subject of their bunions, or the latest political scandal, or both. What value! It was better than most of the rubbish on the telly today.

Old age pensioners with free bus passes were never lonely. They could travel round Glasgow all day and not only enjoy the mobile circus but star in it as well. Some of them went home exhausted, like old troupers. The amount we have lost because of our manic desire for efficiency is incalculable.

So, Mr Prescott, here is this Great Column's three-point action plan which will both Save the Earth and also help solve the unemployment problem.

1. Make it ridiculously expensive to bring private cars into city centres.
2. Put on lots and lots of buses, which will travel speedily through the freed-up cities.
3. Bring back the all-singing, all-dancing clippies, who will give punters change, and welcome visitors with a smile and a joke.

Deputy Prime Minister, your cheque is in the post. My staff will send you a receipt.

True Confessions of the People's Premier

In these days of public humiliations and dreaded "outings", this Great Column is going to have to face its public in confessional mode. It is necessary to begin with an embarrassing declaration about youthful indiscretions. Are the cameras ready? The lights? Let the sweating commence.

Gulp. Here goes. Give me a glass of water. That's better. Now here is my deposition. When I was about 12 or 13, being raised by wolves and roaming free among the pit bings of Cowdenbeath, I and my pals used to go on shopping expeditions. The only snag was that we didn't have any money to buy things with. (Aye, it was tough in these days, living in cardboard boxes, fighting the dogs for scraps, running around in bare feet, and.....)

Not having cash did not stop us shopping. We would saunter into Woolworths, one of the group would distract the shop lassie, and we would snitch a few items from the counter. Then we would saunter out, past the sign saying "Thank you for shopping at Woolworths", and distribute the spoils, us latter-day Fife Robin Hoods.

We got away with it, and we became bolder. We decided to plan a raid on Dunfermline Woolies. This was really the big-time. The game-plan worked again, and we sloped off with some pocket French dictionaries. Just what every 12-year-old in Cowdenbeath wanted.

You may think that this was stealing. But it wasn't, not on my definition of the word "stealing", the one that my expensive lawyers wrote out for me. I called it "consuming", or "redistributing wealth." Okay?

Why am I telling you all this? First, because after the daily diet of revelations about Bill Clinton, your jaded appetites will need stimulated by something even more sensational. And second, because I am thinking of running for the office of prime minister.

I'm not a member of a political party, but that doesn't matter. I'm going to run as "the People's Premier". Seeing youse are the people, you will vote for me. Clever, eh? I'll fight on the platform of redistribution of wealth, though I'll come down really hard on stealing. I will flog petty pilferers, string 'em up, in fact.

But if I'm running for prime minister, why make this public confession? The reason is that once I announce my candidature, the moral bloodhounds will be out to check out my past, my present and my future. No dark stone will be left unturned. So, I'm getting my retaliation in first.

But, I hear you cry plaintively, you haven't told us whether you were caught and punished after your "shopping" expeditions, and whether your career in crime extended to taking part in the Great Train Robbery? You may then inquire: is all that stuff about pilfering really true? And are you really going to run for premier?

Okay, let me make yet another confession. I made up that stuff about being prime minister. It strikes me that no one with any sense nowadays will run for high office. Bill Clinton is an extreme case, since he has wounded himself so spectacularly and so publicly, but how many people would care to have their lives trawled over under the glare of camera lights? In most people's dark inner cupboards there are a few skeletons waiting to clatter out in the most embarrassing fashion – what the liturgy calls "sins of omission and commission."

When John Major was prime minister, a youthful liaison was interred and turned into screaming headlines. His own family's love lives were put under the spotlight. When Tony Blair became leader of the Labour Party, tabloid journalists were out in force, going over his past. Former teenage girl friends and classmates were tracked down, in the hope of turning up sensational news of even a youthful back row fumble. If he is still in office when his children are teenagers, you can be sure that every relationship of theirs will be under scrutiny, with cheque book at the ready to unloosen tongues. This is a very high price to pay for political power.

Blair passed the scrutiny tests. With the connivance of his own spin doctors, he was then built up into a kind of superman. That is when the new set of troubles start. The sight of a person continually walking on the political waters eventually becomes boring. The sport is to gun him down. If things go wrong, the anger knows no bounds. Superman becomes Supervillain.

None of this makes for good government. Why should any person of ability put him or herself forward for public office when they know that their life will be raked over, and that their family will be compelled to live out private agonies in the public spotlight?

It is a strange paradox that at a time when sexual mores are changing so much, the private lives of public figures should come in for such close scrutiny. The editors who sit in judgement are not all conspicuous examples of moral rectitude.

If we only want people who have lived faultless lives to represent us then we will be ruled by John Gummers. If we turn ferociously on politicians because they fail to deliver the whole package of human happiness, we condemn ourselves to leadership of stunning mediocrity. If we encourage a political culture of blame which pretends that every problem is solvable, we tread a wheel of perpetual disappointment. If we support the slavering investigators of private lives, we get the politics we deserve.

Archbishop William Temple was berated by a lady about the indiscretions of some Anglican priests. When she demanded to know why the quality of priests was so low, the Archbishop looked his questioner in the eye and replied, "Because we only have the laity to choose from."

By the way, I didn't get caught. If any of Fife's finest are reading this, I will come quietly. As for the Great Train Robbery, my lips are sealed.

Political Messiah on Mission Impossible

It has to be one of the quotes of the year. "With a sex maniac in the White House and an alcoholic in the Kremlin, isn't it lucky we've got Jesus Christ in Downing Street?" It was uttered, apparently, by a visitor to No 10, and as a shorthand summing-up of the current world political scene it has a lot going for it.

Tony is Coming Home, but it really feels as if he hasn't been away. The Holy Couple have been strolling hand in hand across the front pages of the British press, with Tuscany and the Leaning Tower of Pisa as lucky backdrop. Despite Kosovo, Belfast and all the rest, the ever-present smile is still in place. Strawberry Fields forever. There is something worryingly transcendent about Tony Blair. *Touch me not, for I am not yet ascended to my Father.* Oh dear.

I'm glad he's had a holiday, and I hope it's been a good one. He deserves it. He is a very hard-working premier. Wherever there is a crisis, he is there: wherever two or three are gathered in his name he is in the midst of them, hollow-eyed through lack of sleep, but smiling, smiling. This is what worries me.

On the surface, the smile is that of a relaxed man, but a closer examination reveals small, giveaway signs of strain. That itself is not surprising. Nor is the fact that the young prime minister has aged in office. What is disturbing is the insatiable need to project mastery and success at all times and in all circumstances.

How can I tease out the unease I feel? Blair is a manifestly decent man with good instincts. We could have a great deal worse. Indeed, we have had. Prime Minister for a time, maybe, but I definitely don't want Tony as Messiah. I'd rather not have him out there, at all times of the day and night, bearing the sins of the world. Save us, please, from photo-opportunity stigmata.

Nor do I want a driven, workaholic prime minister. Old handbagging Boadicea herself got by on four hours sleep a night, and she created a fair bit of havoc in the far-too-many hours in which she was zealously awake. (Surely somebody in her cabinet should have been given the role of chloroforming her or jabbing her with a temazapan-tipped umbrella every day?)

It is all right for God to neither slumber nor sleep – though even a knackered Deity needed a kip at the weekend after creating the world and stuff – but Maggie and Tony are mere mortals, despite briefings to the contrary. Ronald Reagan, the Acting President, read the biblical script wrong as usual and thought that every day was the sabbath. (It was once memorably said of Reagan by a White House insider that a particular crisis had given the President "many a sleepless afternoon". There immediately followed much angstful discussion about how possible it was to feel secure when the most powerful figure in the world spent so much time sleeping, or in a dwam. I don't know about you, but I always felt much more secure when President Reagan was tucked up in bed. I felt happier in the knowledge that so many of the President's waking hours were spent asleep, if you know what I mean. It was when he was awake and walking about the face of the earth that I got scared.)

What is much more dangerous than a sleeping President or Prime Minister is an overactive and messianic one. Political leaders are now expected to be perpetually charismatic, forceful, dynamic – and never tired. Not only must they be awake in the afternoons, they are expected to be awake for most of the night as well as they toil selflessly on our behalf. The demand that our leaders should work night and day, frantically running around solving every problem, is part of our demented work-culture. It is very dangerous and destructive, and should be discouraged wherever possible. We do not permit drivers of juggernauts to take to the roads when they are tired. It is no more in our interests that drained political leaders have their hands on the national levers of power – or their fingers on the nuclear buttons – than it is that our lives should be in the care of worn-out junior doctors.

Not only does Blair have the natural demands of high office, but he has created a whole extra raft of them. A further self-inflicted pressure is that he and his advisers connive with the image-based Superman nonsense. The red lights should be flashing: exhausted leaders with make-up and a mission find it hard to tolerate criticism.

The revolution, it seems, requires continual hype, intervention and sermonettes. All this worthiness is very wearying. One is reminded of C.S. Lewis's description of a woman of his acquaintance: "She lived for others, and you could tell who the others were by their hunted look."

But my unease is wider still: it has to do not just with driven leaders, but with a driven culture. Every business or corporation or even family nowadays apparently needs to have a "mission statement". Look, as our blessed leader is wont to say: when we start using messianic language to describe everyday work, we are all in serious trouble. We are confusing categories that should only be confused at our peril.

As the desacralising of the world continues apace, we need, it seems, new gods. What we end up with are serial celebrity idols with beautiful garments and clay feet. But behind them lurks the true Moloch, the impersonal market-forces god which brooks no rivals and demands that even reluctant devotees at the golden shrine work longer and longer hours, even to the destruction of their families.

The gleaming, shining Tony is, I fear, ultimately in thrall to this idol. Even when he has been on holiday there have been stagey, ethereal, photo-opportunities and meetings. I worry that the promised land to which he is so keen to march us is one in which the ever-demanding, voracious Moloch will reign unchecked. Its fat priesthood will live in unparalleled luxury while the poor of the world starve. Tony Blair is not the man to mount a serious challenge to this global unelected hierarchy of wealth and power. That perpetual smile indicates a man who wants, deep down, to be popular. Warm words do not a prophet make.

The myth is that hedonism is rampant: the truth is that most people are too knackered or insecure to participate in the supposed national orgy. Either that, or they are unemployed and can't afford to go to the party. Britain has the longest working hours in Europe, and people at work spend a lot of time looking over their shoulder, afraid even to be ill in case they lose their employment. The rise in chronic fatigue, sexual impotence, and diseases which attack depleted immune systems is probably not unrelated to these trends. If we spend longer and longer hours at work, under more and more burn-out pressure – while people without work gaze apathetically at us through the windows – we need leaders who will challenge the current global principalities and powers.

Political leaders who are compelled to "act" energetically but are internally running on empty are dangerous people. If the Scottish parliament replicates this workaholic macho political lifestyle it will be a dismal failure. The sight of Donald Dewar on two hours of sleep will frighten not just the weans, but all normal adults. We want leaders who will tackle this pathological culture, not embody it.

What we definitely do not need is an all-singing, all-dancing, all-smiling, walking-on-water presidential superstar who pretends that he is above politics, a missionary who wants us all to sing from the same oppressive hymnsheet. Welcome home, Tony.

These Proddy and Catholic Buddhists are pretty good Christians

The sleek car moves through the rolling countryside, the sun glinting on the bonnet. The grass and the trees are lush green in this captivating Borders landscape. We pass through rugby town after rugby town, thinking out loud that from these places there came sturdy farmers who, only a matter of weeks ago, went to the Stade de France and beat the favourites in a thrilling encounter, then gained the Five Nations trophy.

The man at the wheel is a journalist friend. He has borrowed a car belonging to a former girl friend, smooth, with pop-up headlamps (the car, that is). It seems a little incongruous for our pilgrimage. I'm on the intellectual trail of Soren Kierkegaard, Denmark's tortured philosophical and theological genius. There is a physical trail, too: the University of Edinburgh, the Scottish Parliament on the Mound, the General Assembly of the Church of Scotland in unfamiliar high-tech surroundings; and heading now for another institution in the new Scotland.

The car moves quickly along the winding road, and suddenly, as we turn a corner, we see what we are looking for. Standing proudly in the richly wooded Presbyterian landscape is a Buddhist temple, its golden roof reflecting the rays of the warm sun. This is Scotland on the edge of the second Millennium – a fledgling parliament, a displaced and disorientated national Kirk, gleaming mosques in Glasgow, and a thriving Tibetan Buddhist monastery in the Borders.

The connections between Kierkegaard's view of knowledge, the Buddhist understanding of reality, and the threads of the pluralist, fragmented postmodern philosophies which now silently provide the deep structure for so much of the contemporary Western human condition are fascinating ones, but not necessarily the stuff of a Thursday morning column. What this journey is clarifying, though, is that the current institutional changes in Scotland are tokens of more fundamental subterranean shifts. The old Scotland is dying, and what is taking its place is very, very uncertain. These are exciting times in which to be alive.

Samye Ling is the first Tibetan Buddhist centre in the West. Established in 1967 in a country house, it has grown to accommodate 100 monks, nuns and lay people. Its origins rest on the vision of two people. Dr Akong Rinpoche spends a lot of his time abroad, mainly in Tibet, and he brings some of the best of the Tibetan teachers to the Scottish Borders. His co-founder, the abbot, Lama Yeshe Losal, is the retreat master, dealing with the many visitors to Samye Ling. He supervises the retreats of those who go into complete seclusion for three years, three months and three days – most of them Scots who emerge blinking to find that Princess Diana has been killed in a car crash, Britain now has a Labour government, Scotland has its own parliament, NATO has been waging a war in the Balkans, Northern Ireland has an uneasy peace, and Rangers and Celtic are still at war. Some leave the retreat early, fearing breakdown if they explore any more dark corners of their life; others leave with a serenity which nothing can touch.

I remove my shoes to go into the temple, where people are meditating. As I get my bearings, I sense that the atmosphere is reverential, yet with something different around the edges. What is it? Ah, yes, I realise. There is humour in the place. This Buddhist temple is a monument of holiness, and also a great Scottish-Tibetan theatre of the absurd. You feel things could move from the mystical to the Monty Python in seconds. The ironic Kierkegaard would have understood. On the whole, Christians take themselves pretty seriously. As do Muslims. Jews and Buddhists have by far the best lines in self-deprecating humour.

There are young monks around. What startles me is their west of Scotland accents. I discuss this next day with the administrator to the Abbot, who tells me that quite a number are trying to come off drugs. They don't have to be people of a great religious or intellectual history to be accepted – they take vows for a year in the first instance.

For some the regime is too hard, or they can't do without the needle, so they head back home. Others find something better than drugs, and much less destructive. Lives are changed by a therapy of work and worship. I have seen this kind of thing before. Iona. These Proddy and Catholic Buddhists are pretty good Christians, if you know what I mean.

The administrator is an attractive woman, shaved head, robes. Her mother is a kirk elder in Perthshire. In the office full of Buddhas and computers, she explains how the order is establishing a foundation on Holy Island.

Yes, old Scotia is changing. At a time when the historic Protestant and Catholic churches, exhausted and grey after centuries of Pyrrhic struggles, look on in bewilderment as the punters head rapidly for the exits, secular Scotland restlessly looks elsewhere for spiritual nourishment. And Kierkegaard, that perceptive pre-modern postmodernist, glances wryly over from Denmark and says to Scottish Christendom, you've had it coming pal.

Who will listen to the voices of the poor?

It is time to ask the question again: what exactly is a Scottish parliament for? Or, to put it another way, to whom will it make a difference?

I have a strong feeling about this. The strength of that feeling is based on two things – the depth of a recurrent UK scandal, and personal experience. If the Scottish parliament is largely about national cheer-leading and flag-waving, it will be a waste of space and money.

The scandal? The fact that we have known for years that people in poorer areas of our land die considerably younger than those in the more affluent parts. Report after report has borne out this simple, brutal fact. Each investigation over the years has had its five minutes of publicity, and is then forgotten, until the next one comes along. We have no excuses. We know. We have seen the deadly figures for the housing schemes and inner city areas. They tell us, for instance, that average life expectancy in Drumchapel is substantially less than in neighbouring Bearsden. No honeyed words can obliterate the graffiti of disease and death.

This is by no means simply a central belt issue. The most recent report was on Aberdeen. "In Aberdeen, like every other city in Scotland," it states, "the gap in health status and life expectancy between the rich and the poor has widened over the last two decades. Patterns of death and illness are strongly associated with patterns of deprivation."

In other words: in our land of plenty, poverty kills. We know about the Third World abroad. But there is a Fourth World on our own doorstep – a shadowy world of poverty, indebtedness, disease and low life expectancy. The real measure of a Scottish parliament will be how well it deals with that Scottish Fourth World. And no, the problems will not be solved by persuading people to eat more apples and muesli.

I mentioned personal experience. In eight years of living and working in Easterhouse I saw these infernal statistics in flesh and blood, in doctors' surgeries, in hospital wards and at crematoria; and also the tremendous spirit of survivors.

The Labour government has acknowledged the problem, and has appointed Alistair Darling to oversee the tackling of poverty and social exclusion. "Fifty years on," he says, "a child can still be born poor, live poor and die poor." Too right. But does Labour have the will to deal with the matter in radical ways that may cause electoral pain?

A priority for the Scottish parliament should be to listen to the poor of Scotland, and make attendance at the hearings mandatory for all MSPs. One of the bodies which has done most to encourage the voices of the poor in Scotland to be heard is the Glasgow Braendam Link. It enables families under severe pressure to have a break at Braendam House near Stirling, and helps them look at their situation.

The group has a tremendous track record over many years, and it is sad that the project itself is having to scrabble around for funds simply to stay alive.
The Braendam Link's outstanding Project Co-ordinator,

Molly Harvey, should be a key witness at the parliamentary hearings. Another is Bob Holman, former Professor of Social Administration at Bath University, who has lived in Easterhouse for years as part of a neighbourhood project. Bob, like Molly Harvey, works alongside the poor without being patronising.

His latest book, *Faith in the Poor* (Lion, £16.99) should be mailed to all MSPs. What he has done is to provide a platform for seven Easterhouse residents to spell out what it feels like to be poor and powerless in Scotland today.

Most of all, poor people themselves should have the opportunity to address the parliamentarians directly. The notion that all poverty is caused by booze, fecklessness and unwillingness to work is a self-serving myth – a myth which can be exploded only by listening to, and cross-examining, a range of people caught up in debilitating poverty.

If the poverty trap is clamped firm, nothing fundamental will have changed in Scotland. And if the majority of Scots, who are comparatively well off, are encouraged to ignore the fact that the neighbours over the high wall experience continued poverty of opportunity and die earlier, then we may well be wealthier, but we will be diminished as a people as well.

This year's DAFTA Awards

For the last few months or so, there seems to have been a film or theatre award every week. Oscars, BAFTA awards, British Film Industry awards: the show goes on, and on. Hardly a day goes by without someone collecting an award for doing the eyebrows on the set of "McGonagle in Love", and staggering towards the microphone, full of emotion, to thank their producer, mother, father, dog, God, postman or crystal pendant. How many sobbing luvvies can one take, for heaven's sake?

If it's not the Hollywood awards (Best Film, Best Actor, Best Burger Maker, Best Moustache Shampooer) it's the British, or Scottish, or Fife, or Lochgelly Awards. The format is the same – the tension, the losers spitting nails while trying to feign goodwill, the toe-curling acceptance speeches by the winners, and the disinterment of some sillicone-enhanced crone to receive a Lifetime Achievement Award. All to violins.

This column fails to see why it should be excluded from this elevating process. It has therefore decided to institute the annual DAFTA Awards, to celebrate the most stupid things done during the last year. I have had special gold statuettes of Cowdenbeath footballers made at colossal expense, and these coveted awards will go to people who have turned failure into an art form.

First up for a DAFTA is the man who went off on a

shopping spree using the stolen credit card belonging to Celtic star Henrik Larsson. If you're going to defraud, then using the card of one of the most photographed celebrities in the country isn't the cleverest way of going about it. The sheriff was so amazed by the case that he ordered the accused to appear before him in person to see how much the short-haired Scot resembled the Swedish dreadlocked striker. Chances are the man in the courtroom who will most resemble Larsson will be the sheriff himself, since lawmen wear ringlets-of-badger's-bum on their daft wee heids when they are dispensing justice. The encounter promises to be pure Scottish theatre of the most surreal kind.

And what about Justin Clark, the unfortunate man who stole a pager from a car? David Withers, the car owner, sent the thief a message on the pager congratulating him on winning £500 in a competition, and inviting him to ring in to claim the prize. When the thief obligingly telephoned, Withers agreed to meet him. Go straight to jail. Do not pass Go.

A very strong candidate for a DAFTA is accountant Werner Fuks of Vienna, who destroyed his house when he discovered mouse droppings on the floor. Utterly obsessed, Fuks tore his kitchen apart, pulled up his carpets and ripped open his furniture in his bid to find the offending creature. Completely maddened, he began pulling down the ceilings. Neighbours became alarmed by the noise, and phoned the police. Fuks was taken away in an ambulance with the victorious moose still loose aboot his hoose.

Spare a thought for an Australian vicar, the Reverend Timothy Peet. When his car broke down outside a pub in Sydney, he went inside to get help. As soon as he went in the door, 30 drunken women ran at him, screaming, "It's the vicargram! Get 'em off!" They forced him on to a stage to perform a "dirty show". It certainly made a change from

DAFTA

a douce wee talk on "Women in the Bible" at the WRI. The ladies realised their mistake when the real vicargram arrived 20 minutes later. They kindly returned the genuine clergyman's clothes and dog collar and gave his car a push start.

There's more! This ever-vigilant column with its informers in every part of the known world and in some parts of the unknown world, can report to you that fancy dress partygoer Francisco Rivera, 26, wore his gorilla outfit out on the streets in Pisa and was shot with tranquiliser darts by local zoo keepers. Even before the Daily Record could mount a campaign to save the unconscious gorilla, Francisco woke up in time to explain that he was actually a human being of sorts.

Out of all the DAFTA candidates, my chosen panel of distinguished experts on madness – Professors D. Dewar, D. McLetchie, A. Salmond and J. Wallace – have decided that the top award should go to Mr Alan Dustings, a 45-year old Canadian fisherman whose story is almost too painful to narrate. You see, the poor man was admitted to hospital with a trout on his penis. How did it all go pear-shaped, so to speak?

"Because it was a lovely day, and no one was around, I'd gone naked," he explained. "I reeled in a whopper of a trout, but as I removed the hook, the fish clamped its jaws around my tackle. Frantic tugging proved hopeless. It was rather humiliating. The nurses wouldn't stop laughing."

I hope that none of the readers of this ennobling column are laughing at the misfortunes of this poor man. At least he will have a golden statuette of a Cowdenbeath footballer on his mantlepiece to console him, as he tucks into his trout. Next year, may I sternly remind you, it could be you.

Pinochet: an open letter to the Home Secretary

Dear Mr Straw, D-Day is approaching, and I do not envy you your task. Within a few days, you must decide whether to use your discretionary powers to permit General Augusto Pinochet to return home to Chile, or to let the law take its course and allow extradition proceedings to go ahead. Whatever decision you make you will be reviled by powerful people. That goes with the territory.

You will have been besieged with advice. Intensive representations have already been made at the highest political level, and you have been lobbied by various interest groups. You will have piles of letters and faxes in your in-tray; you will also have received lots of late-night telephone calls, as well as special pleadings whispered in your ear. You are in a lonely place.

The case for allowing the General to return home in peace is an overwhelming one. He is 83 years old, and not in very robust health. Democracy in Chile is somewhat precarious. Britain has important trading links with Chile, and jobs could be at stake. Not only that, there lurks a further difficult question: why stop with Augusto Pinochet? If you allow the General to be extradited, surely the floodgates of international prosecutions will open?
You must have wished the Law Lords had voted differently,

and taken the matter out of your hands.

But they didn't, Mr Straw; and you now have to decide. The heat in your political kitchen must be at boiling point.

May I presume to offer you yet another unsolicited piece of advice? It is this: I believe that you should set aside the powerful arguments for aborting the legal process and direct that General Pinochet, like lesser mortals, should face the consequences of his actions.

Why? Because of *los Desaparecidos,* the Disappeared. Their ghostly voices seek justice. Their blood cries up from the ground. Behind all the noisy argument about trade, political balance and British-Chilean relationships, the volume of these whispered prayers must be turned up – and when they are heard, there can only be one verdict. Let the General stand trial.

Last week, on television, I saw an old man almost beside himself with rage. He had been a British prisoner-of-war in a Japanese concentration camp, and he had been subjected to unspeakable things. He and his fellow survivors simply wanted acknowledgement of what had been done to them and their friends who had perished. They wanted justice, but it was denied them. The Japanese judges did not even give a respectful hearing to their testimony. The elderly Briton shouted through tears: "You may be prosperous, but how can you live with yourselves if you deny people justice?" Afterwards, a smooth Japanese ambassador said that it was time to put all these unfortunate things behind them and look to the future.

No, no, no. It cannot be. The old, tired, prisoner-of-war was right. If there is no justice, no truth-facing, the bread stored in the prosperous freezers becomes what the Bible calls "the bread of tears." It is not possible to move on the future with any integrity if the past has not been honestly dealt with. The truth has to be told.

Britain has been helping to bring some of the ethnic-cleansers of Bosnia to judgment. The brutalised, tortured, dead victims have had their ghostly day in court, and no living human being could remain unaffected.

It may be argued that General Pinochet should be released on compassionate grounds. Listen: suppose an 82-year-old man called Thomas Vogel had been found in a house in Guatemala some years back. Suppose he had had comprehensive plastic surgery. Suppose his real name was Adolf Hitler. Would we say that he should not stand trial, on compassionate grounds?

What about compassion for the people tortured in Pinochet's Chile? What about the relatives of the slaughtered and the vanished ones? Where is the compassion for them?

There is a place for compassion. In any fair legal system, mitigating circumstances are taken into account and mercy may be shown – but that is only after the truth has been told. To pre-empt the whole process is to abort justice, and justice has to be disinterested. It must apply to the greatest as to the least.

It is a matter of historical record, not of propaganda, that during General Pinochet's 17-year rule, thousands of people were abducted and cruelly tortured and killed. No one knows where many of them are buried. Who will speak for them in the highest courts of the land?

Questions about trade and the future of democracy in Chile are not trivial. British relations with Chile are also important. But now, the voices of the *Desaparecidos* must take precedence. Chile must face its past, and Augusto Pinochet must face his accusers.

This line of argument will be regarded by some people as moralising sentimentality. So be it. There should no hiding place for people who commit crimes against humanity, whether of the Right or the Left, whether South

American, African, East European or British. General Pinochet thought he had made himself immune from prosecution by appointing himself a Life Senator of Chile. Why should there be a law for the rich and powerful, and a law for the poor? Why should the General, literally, get away with murder?

As we approach the 50th anniversary of the signing of the Universal Declaration of Human Rights, the unambiguous words of Lord Nichols - no radical - serve notice on despots: "No one, not even a head of state, should get away with abhorrent crimes." (Nor for that matter should Sinn Fein/IRA - responsible for other "Disappeared" - or bent British interrogators in dark Ulster police cells.)

Mr Straw, judgment day is at hand. Put aside the piles of paper, and listen. Listen intently to the voices of the unquiet dead. Then reach for your pen.

Hope for healing in this tragic land

I love this land, this beautiful land. Its scenery can be breathtaking, its people warm and generous and hospitable and humorous. Yet at times it can seem cursed, fated, a theatre of atavistic hatred.

I've been many times to Ireland: to Donegal, to Belfast, to the mountains of Mourne, to Dublin. And I'm back in Belfast, driving along the Newtonards Road, travelling in the direction of Stormont, venue of the peace process. I notice significant little changes. The kerbstones are now painted red, white and blue. It is intended to intimidate. It must have been done – or permitted – by the city fathers.

The whole tragedy which binds Ireland to Scotland defies verbal analysis. It defies normal speech, even for a people who delight in words. Prose is no use, too prosaic. It has to be stammering poetry, even though poetry can't come remotely near, either.

I close my eyes and call to mind some of the participants in the peace process. Why do so many of the Loyalist leaders sound like angry, frightening, frightened bullfrogs. What kind of osmosis is going on? I think of the defiant, florid man I went to hear perform in his Belfast temple-theatre.

He stands his ground – and even yours –
deploring damning roaring ranting

and says (thank God) it's all for love
of Christ (but not His holy mother
if you understand).

His howl is howled (should it be fluted?)
as he wades the bloody river
there is nothing muted in this Captain
Furious. His aye is for an aye, his nay
means never; strong his right arm to smite
luxurious ease, his bullish face set hard
against deceitful Catholic charm
and weasel Southern comfort.
The wages of sin is death, is death;
there will be No Surrender.
The sash his father wore
is made of heavy chunks of mail,
a binding Orange armoured suit
of lore which makes him mobile
as a clanking Goliath –
invulnerable to slings
and arrows of outrageous
truth – or a lumbering Craigavon centre half.
When that day comes, he will be lifted
high on luminous white steed,
drawing all men unto him. All roads will lead
to Paisley in the Irish unfree state.

The prime minister has come and gone, shaking hands with the unshakeable, and being jostled for his pains. Why do so many of the Nationalist leaders look so shifty, so untrustworthy, so chilling?

The Toiseach twitches at the Liffey bar.
Asked what he really thinks, he orders
a united Ireland (but in a whisper,
with a wink) and tries to laugh

when he is served a Bloody Mary. Blessed art thou
among drinks, the bearded barman quips,
crossing and double-crossing himself
with enigma. The smile which plays
around the tender's lips is taut,
the cocktail-maker's eyes as cold
as northern seas. He knows his pay day
has come close, he's counting now,
his tips have bought the wages of Sinn
Fein, as sure as death: while earnest crimson
bishops sweat in holy fury day and night
(for the love of Christ and his virgin mother)
to cleanse the green and pleasant land
of condoms.

There are words of hope, but the people seem resigned, not wanting to hope too much. I think of the words of photographer Don McCullin, who has been covering the world's tragedies over the last 20 years. "I recorded it all as history unfolding, believing that this could never happen again but it has, and it will. I am under no illusions now. Humanity will go on suffering till the end of time."

Is there any sign of a Mandela, a de Klerk? Can there be a miracle at Christmas?

Along the gloaming border road
the bleeding crosses bleed
and bleed and bleed.
And in the city still strung high
with lights and fading messages of peace,
goodwill, red-handed magi ride the Falls
on death-white steeds to meet apocalyptic fate
in 1690 on crumbling gable walls – Veni, veni,
Immanuel. Even now come late, come late.

It seems that Ireland will have to give up religion before it can become Christian. Yet given its history, a renewed religious symbolism will have to be part of the healing of the land. Can a new, twisted but transforming thing be born out of unspeakable suffering in a bloodied Belfast cradle?

And from the appointed tenemental room
come shrieks of hell and fits of desperate loss.
Blessed art thou among bloody
women, the sardonic midwife spits
with sign of cross in bitter theatre.
For the love of Christ! the Shankhill
schoolgirl howls, too often battered
and abused to be a holy mother. She bleeds
and bleeds and bleeds and labours
to bring forth a baby, blue,
red bloodlines on his palms. Behold
your man, a tiny Protestant equipped
with stigmata.

I drive back down the Newtonards Road, red, white, and blue. I love this land: this beautiful, sainted tragic land.

Pint-sized Viking dances away to freedom

For me, he was the star of the Festival, this primary school Viking hero. For reasons which will become obvious, I will not name him.

Since its inception, the St Magnus Festival has established an astonishing track record. Its founding fathers – the composer Sir Peter Maxwell Davies and poet George Mackay Brown – have attracted big names in music, drama and literature to Orkney, including Eleanor Bron, Julian Bream, Andre Previn, Vladimir Ashkenazy, Isaac Stern, Evelyn Glennie, Tommy Smith, Tom Fleming, Sorley MacLean, Norman McCaig, Seamus Heaney, Brian McCabe and Iain Crichton Smith.

Under the shrewd artistic direction of Maxwell Davies, and then of Glenys Hughes – along with her late husband Dick, of fond memory – the Festival has also commissioned new works by young 'unknown' composers who have gone on to make a name for themselves, such as Judith Weir and James MacMillan.

When the star musicians and poets come to Orkney, they often stay in the homes of local people. Big name artists mingle with the locals in the streets and pubs. There is not a bed to be had in Kirkwall, as the town expands to hold the visitors from all over the world, drawn to this unique community event.

And it's all been worth it, all 21 years of it, for this primary school kid. But I'll come to him later.

The Festival marked its coming-of-age with a huge multi-media performance based on the Orkneyinga Saga, the stories of the bloodthirsty Viking earls of Orkney. The stories were played out simultaneously at three historic Kirkwall sites, before the finale in St Magnus Cathedral.

As the person commissioned to write the script, I found myself working in collaboration with some of the most creative people I've ever met – composer Steve King, choreographer Andy Howitt, and aerial artist Jonothan Campbell, who returned to his childhood home to teach Orcadian youngsters some stunning skills. And behind it all, the presiding genius of Penny Aberdein, the Stromness-based director who conceived the idea and masterminded the production with a brilliant touch.

On the opening night, I found myself as awed as *Herald* arts critic Michael Tumelty by the sheer scale and passion of the production. For me, there were two heart-stopping moments. Magnus, in a dripping red coat, seemed to embrace Lifolf, his executioner (a Kirkwall Grammar School pupil, high on menacing stilts) as he received the fatal blow, then lay in deep silence, stretched out dramatically in front of the Cathedral.

Then into the Viking temple itself, where Magnus was slowly and majestically borne the length of the nave, while the choir in the triforium sang an atmospheric requiem in magnificent dissonance. ("Does the choir know they are singing out of tune?" whispered one awe-struck primary school child.)

What was remarkable was that all of the near-300 participants in the production were Orkney-based. There were no imported actors, dancers, singers or musicians. Children as young as seven danced and mimed the story of the martyrdom of Magnus in front of the Cathedral – some of them in the company of their dancing mothers! Few of these parents had ever danced before, other than on Saturday nights at the disco in Matchmakers.

Steve King taught primary school kids how to master handbells in order to provide the atmospheric musical background for St Rognvald's sea journey to Jerusalem, the words sung by Ishbel Fraser, a young Orcadian of great purity of tone who sings Sunday by Sunday at the Kirkwall Salvation Army Hall. Under the tutelage of Jonothan Campbell, pupils at Kirkwall Grammar School (their Rector, Eric Sinclair, was one of the leading actors) learned how to be spooky, lurking Viking fates on confident stilts.

What the audience witnessed was a community acting, speaking, dancing, singing its own history. What is more, the cast did it not in the kind of way which produces kindly, condescending applause – they did it in ways which took the breath away. What we also saw was the exciting possibilities which develop when adults are prepared to act as mentors for children and encourage natural talents to blossom.

Sir Peter Maxwell Davies was visibly moved by the whole event. The only sadness was that George Mackay Brown was not alive in the flesh to witness this happening in and around his beloved Cathedral.

The arts can change lives. I have seen it with my own eyes in two communities I have lived in – Easterhouse and Orkney. Excellence does not have to walk hand in hand with elitism. Young people and adults can find new confidence as they discover talents they did not dream they possessed.

What about the lad I spoke of? When Andy Howitt was working with primary school kids, teaching them to dance, one boy proved to be a natural. He exulted in the movement. When Andy pointed this out, the boy's teacher was surprised and touched. "He's a very difficult boy," she said quietly, out of pained experience. When Andy held a voluntary advanced dancing class on the Saturday, the "difficult boy" was first in the queue. At last he had found something he could do, and do well.

So, there he was, in front of St Magnus Cathedral, doing the swooping dance of a Viking earl – the Difficult Boy showing them how it's done, dancing his heart out in front of his admiring peers. His life will never be the same.

This St Magnus Festival is worth it. Worth it for the dead departed, George Mackay Brown and Dick Hughes. Worth it for Vladimir Ashkenazy and Isaac Stern. Worth it for Judith Weir and James MacMillan.

But above all, worth it for the swirling, exultant pint-size Unknown Viking Warrior, dancing his way to freedom.

Trapped in Purgatory by heavenly new computers

Anglian Water has had to apologise for sending a letter to the late Audrey Hayler. It began, believe it or not, "Dear Mrs Deceased, we aim to make life easier again." I would guess that making life easier for their former customer is beyond the powers even of Anglian Water. Another woman, the late Margaret Malone, from Co. Carlow, Ireland, was recently informed that her name was being removed from the electoral register because she was dead. The letter advised the woman, who died three years ago, that if she wished to dispute the decision she should notify the council right away.

Computerised mailings are hazardous. Gas and electricity bills telling customers that they owe £3m for the quarter can have terminal consequences. Then, presumably, the organisation can write, "Dear Mr Deceased, we note from our records that you still owe us £3m. Please pay up immediately. Have a nice day!" At the bottom of the letter to the incinerated addressee will be some ghastly "mission slogan" such as Provincial Power – keeping you hot all day. Burn on, MacDuff!

I have a shuddering aversion to the messages which come from the likes of *Readers Digest.* They are prime examples of the fake-personal computer style.

"Congratulations Mr Ferguson! You have been selected to take part in the next stage of our Prize Draw, the first prize of which is a new Mercedes car! We want to tell you, Mr Ferguson, that only one in eight households in your neighbourhood has been selected to take part in this draw! Can you not just imagine, Mr Ferguson, your sparkling new Mercedes sitting outside your home in Berstane Road, Kirkwall?"

Frankly, no. What I can imagine is chloroforming the writer of the letter in the name of humanity. Does he or she really think that we are all so thick as to believe that we are being addressed personally, just because our name is scattered liberally through the text? You would have to be less up to speed than a Lochgelly hedgehog with dementia not to know that a computer is churning out this brain-endangering drivel. There is something dispiriting about these ubiquitous ersatz-personal computer-generated messages. I don't know about you, but when the mail comes in the morning, with its usual pile of computerised addresses, I fall upon any letter with a hand-written address on the envelope.

Computers were supposed to usher in the age of the paperless office. In fact, all they have done is generate pile upon pile of paperwork. They would, we were told, help to create the new, caring, jobsharing society, in which people would work more civilised hours. The reality is that they are helping to accelerate an increasingly driven society.

Every government department and business seems to be reorganising its life around new computer systems. "I was to learn later in life that we tend to meet any new situation by reorganising; and a wonderful method it can be for creating the illusion of progress while producing confusion, inefficiency and demoralisation" – these words penned by Petronius Arbiter in 60 AD should be read aloud at the start of every meeting held to discuss a new computer system.

The other day I phoned to book a driving test for my

son. I was told to call back, as the computer system had just crashed. Many pensioners have been without benefits for some weeks because the new computer system recording Nation Insurance payments developed more than 1500 faults. A major new system at the DSS is now 18 months overdue, and will cost the taxpayer an extra £10m. People can't get passports because the system has gone down the tubes.

Computers have their uses, but the apparently unchallengeable computer-as-liberator ideology is a god that has failed. There are many zealous worshippers at its shrine – and there is no bore quite as boring as a computer bore – but its tedious and broken liturgies will not usher in the new kingdom.

Now, we are told, a computer is being developed which will search for God. And when it has located the heavenly spheres, what will the machine do? It will no doubt go on automatic pilot and spew out "personal" letters. "Congratulations Mr Christ! You have been selected to take part in the next stage of our Christmas Draw, the first prize of which is a new Mercedes car! We want to tell you, Mr Christ, that only one in eight households in your neighbourhood has been selected! Can you not just imagine, Mr Christ, your sparkling new Mercedes sitting outside your home at Pearly Gates Road! You will be the envy of your neighbours!"

The non-acquisitive Buddha will shrug his shoulders and laugh at it all. And outside the gates, the vast queues of hopeful punters will be told by St Peter that they'll have to wait for several eternities. Having been brought up on the old-fashioned ledger, he has pressed the wrong button on the newly installed computer system – described in the glossy advert as "heavenly" – and has wiped out the complete celestial database.

The people on the sidelines support their living patron saint

Did you know that Aung San Suu Kyi, brave leader of the Burmese opposition party, is a Cowdenbeath supporter? No, this isn't an April Fool. She has never visited Central Park as far as I am aware, but there is strong evidence to suggest that news of the fortunes of the Blue Brazil – currently languishing as usual at the foot of the Scottish Third Division – is not entirely absent from her consciousness.

Aung San Suu Kyi is an astonishing person, one of the most impressive women in the world. I've been a fan of hers for a long time. When she married Dr Michael Aris 27 years ago, the couple made a pact that if it were the right thing to do, she would return to Burma. She did so in 1988, with Michael's full support. Ever since her National League for Democracy won a landslide election victory in 1990, Suu Kyi has been either in prison or held under house arrest. She has been courageously critical of the junta's actions, and has repeatedly drawn public attention to their abuse of human rights. In 1991, she was awarded the Nobel Peace prize.

Now that her devoted husband has died of cancer, some people have criticised her for remaining in Burma – now called Myanmar by the junta – and for not being with her family. I wouldn't. It must have been a deeply painful decision for her, but Suu Kyi knew that if she left the country, she would not be allowed back. She is democracy's most potent symbol in that part of the world, and her presence there is an inspiration to many people whose human rights are repeatedly denied. The junta know that if they harm her, there will be a world-wide outcry. Exile would suit the rulers.

But what about this Cowdenbeath nonsense? Two or three years ago, I wrote a book about my home football team and the death of a mining culture, *Black Diamonds and the Blue Brazil.* One day, I received a letter from a lady in London. Her father, Dr Duncan Young, had been a GP in Cowdenbeath in the 1930s, and he took his enthusiastic daughter to all the home games. She was able to cite all the matches and scores.

In the book, I had mentioned that Professor Sir James Black, Nobel prize winner for medicine, was from Cowdenbeath. The writer of the letter, a Mrs Evelyn Aris, proudly told me that her beloved daughter-in-law was a Nobel prize winner – Aung San Suu Kyi, no less. Fantasy mode immediately took over. Did my heroine confuse her bewildered interrogators by reciting the Cowdenbeath scores of 1938, as taught by her Blue Brazil-supporting mother-in-law?

Is the Myanmar Special Branch currently pouring over the confiscated *Black Diamonds and the Blue Brazil,* searching for hidden meanings among the tales of glorious defeat and disaster? (There must have been times when Suu Kyi felt like following the old Cowdenbeath saw, quoted in the book, "If at first you don't succeed, pull the blankets ow'r yer heid." But she didn't, she didn't.)

Back to hard reality. Has her imprisonment been worth it, or is it simply a powerless gesture which has deprived a husband and two twentysomething sons of the physical love of a wife and mother? No doubt, in the long nights, Suu Kyi has repeatedly asked herself that very question. The most agonising choices in life are not between good and evil, but between one good and another. And how many of us have totally unambiguous motives? Purity of heart, said the great Søren Kierkegaard, is to will one thing. But in this case, what is the one thing which should be willed?

The notion of sacrifice for a greater good is deeply embedded in both Christian and Buddhist traditions. Unnecessary sacrifices and masochistic martyrdoms are discouraged, but an unselfish sacrificial act made for the benefit of others is a beautiful gift, one which challenges a hedonistic culture to its very core. To willingly give up a rich and full life for others is a truly awesome thing. Suu Kyi is prepared to do just that.

Tomorrow is Good Friday, the commemoration of the loving sacrifice of Jesus of Nazareth who, even as he was stretched out on a cross, forgave his enemies. Tomorrow at Suu Kyi's home in Rangoon there will be a ceremony in which 53 Buddhist monks (one for each year of Michael's life) will memorialise a very contemporary sacrifice. I find the conjunction of these two signs of austere beauty almost unbearably moving.

Alexander and Kim, the couple's two sons, grieving their father and the absence of their mother, can be deeply proud of both their parents. I hope that they will see the day when their mother is prime minister of a free Burma. There are no guarantees. As for now, they have experienced some deprivations, but they also know that they have been nourished by something which is not entirely of this world.

Might is not always right. Hang in there, Suu Kyi. Many people hold you in their hearts right now. People at the bottom of the world's third divisions look up to you, their most precious supporter, their living patron saint.

Sculpting hope in the place of hatred

This is an everyday tale of murdering folk, violence, vengeance, venomous hatred, books, redemption and hypocrisy: and I saw some of it from the inside. Not the story of Mary Bell, the child murderer whose distinguished biographer, Gitta Sereny, has become a hate figure in the public prints, but of a famous Scot, one James Boyle.

It all happened in the late 1970s when I was a Church of Scotland minister in Easterhouse, Glasgow. I was living with my family in a street filled with big families, many of whom had at least one member boarding out in the Big Hoose, Barlinnie.

I do not tell you this in order to appear heroic, because I certainly did not feel it. I remember in the early hours of one Sunday morning being awakened by a commotion. I looked out of the bedroom window and saw a gang-fight going on. Teenagers were fighting with swords. One lad had a swing at a dog, missed, and the sparks flew up from the street where his sword struck the pavement. I determined that I was not going outside to shed my blood – after all, in a few hours I had a sermon to preach about loving your neighbour. At that moment I knew that whatever else I was, St Francis of Assisi I was not.

What the experience did was to teach me something about the circumstances in which violent crime flourishes. Over eight years, I got to know some of the most frightening and some of the most fantastic people I have ever met. The experience changed my life.

I also learned that the herding of people into ghettos, into urban Sowetos, suited society at large. To stick disadvantaged people together into a reservation with few jobs or facilities, then demonise them, was an effective distancing tactic, one which permitted a denial of responsibility.

Ordinary people, many of whom had had very abusive childhoods and who were struggling for survival, became "evil" in the eyes of those who wanted none of the potential trouble anywhere near their own back yards.

I learned at first hand the gulf between "us" and "them". Some people in the Kirk, quite proud of having one of "us" living among "them", would ask me: "Are you winning?" Winning what, precisely? What I knew for sure was that others were losing, drowning even.

A friend of mine, George Wilson, used to go regularly to the Special Unit at Barlinnie to teach a man serving a life sentence for murder how to look after budgies. It seemed bizarre to me. It gave "I'd like to wring her neck" a new meaning. But no necks were wrung. The violent lifer learned how to care tenderly for budgies. And became more human in the process.

George felt that I should visit. The only problem was that the Special Unit had been declared – by a vote of inmates and staff – a clergy-free zone. George spoke to them persuasively, and they voted. So I became the first meenister to darken the doors of the Special Unit.

I got to know James Boyle – not the kind of man one would choose as Sunday School Superintendent. We talked. He sculpted. He made beautiful and expressive things, did this murderer. He sent me letters. I learned about his background. What would I have become, if I had had his upbringing? I had no answer to that question. Nothing could excuse his crimes. He had been a really hard man, working for loan sharks in Gorbals. But was he evil, the monster the tabloids talked about?

Under the old prison regime, Boyle had attacked prison warders, and covered the walls of his cell with his own excrement. But now that he was being treated as a human being instead of a piece of shit himself, he was making sculpture. The man had a talent.

The tabloids screamed against the Special Unit. When Boyle was allowed out to attend one of his own exhibitions, people went crazy.

What I discovered was that there were powerful people who wanted him to fail, in order to prove their own theories that the likes of Boyle couldn't change. One former Moderator of the General Assembly of the Kirk was vehement in his view that the Special Unit should be shut down forthwith. There were church people who – and I choose my words carefully – wanted Boyle to re-offend.

The sight of a such a notoriously violent man changing was, strangely, too much for some clerics. The reason was that his redemption wasn't according to church formulae. He didn't grovel enough, didn't show enough self-loathing, didn't use the right coded language. Somehow a changed, articulate Boyle was more of a threat than one who lived like a caged animal.

The rage became even worse when Boyle wrote about his experiences. Then when another lifer made a powerful sculpture of a naked Christ, the anger was truly murderous. Christ was the property of the Church, not of evil murderers! And despite the biblical accounts of the crucifixion, the Word-became-flesh was acceptable only if it was androgynous, sanitised and modestly wearing first-century Palestinian Y-fronts.

I cannot justify Boyle's crimes. I cannot justify the crimes of Mary Bell, the child killer who was the daughter of a sado-masochistic prostitute. If it had been my child who was killed, I too would be filled with a murderous rage.

But nor can I justify the creation of urban ghettos, and the monstering and scapegoating of people. As a journalist, I cannot justify the ethics of newspapers which pay vast sums for obscenities then shriek "blood money" at Mary Bell and identify her daughter. As a human being, I cannot justify the lynch mob at the door, nor the populist words of my privileged prime minister.

I do not know the answers: but in my manse there is a special sculpture which is a symbol of hope. And there are desperate people, in Easterhouse and in Barlinnie, who have taught me more than theologians about the meaning of that most precious word, redemption.

Rise of the living dead

The other day, I came across some fascinating information about zombies. Under the heading, "Professor digs up an explanation for nightmare of the living-dead", the story told about some recent research undertaken by Professor Roland Littlewood of the Department of Anthropology and Psychiatry at University College, London, and Dr Chavannes Douyon, an expert based at the Polyclinique Medica in Port-au-Prince.

It seems that zombies – supposedly corpses brought back to life by black magic – are probably people with psychiatric disorders and brain damage. The new research shows that zombies are people whose will, awareness and memory have been stolen by a sorcerer, called a "boko". The victim appears to be dead, and is usually buried in an above-ground tomb. The boko then steals and reanimates the body, and sets it to work as a slave. Up to 1000 zombies are said to be created each year, and they are frequently recognised by the local population.

The researchers believe that the voodoo bokos in Haiti may use poisonous toxins from the puffer fish to induce paralysis, after which the victims are stolen from the tombs.

This research offers stunning new insights into the rise and rise of New Labour. How else can one explain the puritan New Model Army, some of whom were once animated and independent human beings capable of original thinking? They are now “on message”, or “singing from the same hymn sheet” as the ghastly pervasive modern jargon goes. They repeat the same mantras, have the same kind of colour-coded clothes, and don’t speak in public without permission. When they do get permission, the bleeper from the Head Boko tells them what to say. The nightmare of the political living-dead is with us right now.

New Labour have mastered the black voodoo arts, but it may yet prove to be their undoing. Tony Blair says that the Labour Party will have grown up when it has learned to love Peter Mandelson. I think there will have to be quite a few injections from the toxin of the puffer fish before that happens. The party bokos may prefer corporate love-ins to full-blooded party conferences, phoney photo-opportunities to substantial policy, and fully disciplined corpses to fully sentient humans, but unless the power of the bokos is broken we will all become zombiefied.

The continual news manipulation is deeply insulting and – just as bad – deeply boring. The Tory party, which used to be able to rely on the support of the big newspaper magnates, looks as if it will go down the same road. What a dire prospect! The Labour party is a schizophrenic mixture of genuinely decentralising tendency and irritating control freakishness, living in perpetual fear of a drop in popularity ratings. It is already fighting the next election, and its authoritarianism, far from being attractive, is a real turn-off.

We need colour in our politics, not monochrome. Take Tony Banks, the Minister for Sport. How long will he last? For all I know, Tony may be a few substitutes short of a full bench, but he has not yet descended to the netherworlds of newspeak. “When God gave Paul Gascoigne his football talent,” he said, “he took his brain out at the same time.”

Mr Banks is equally trenchant about politics. “I’m

afraid that in the bottom-kissing world of politics in which we live," he says, "it's not what you say, it's who says it."

Banks shoots from the hip. "If you're going to dump your fundamentals, dump your ideology and disown your history, you're going off into the desert without a map. Like Mark bloody Thatcher."

The Labour MP has been amusingly disrepectful about the Head Boko himself.

"I've had a fairly rough time myself," said Mr Banks, after Peter Mandelson had failed to win a place on the Labour Party's National Executive. "If Peter Mandelson ever came out in the daylight he would probably get the same treatment."

He warned MPs who had not voted for Mr Mandelson to carry a clove of garlic for protection. "Do you ever get that scary, scary feeling that there's more than one Peter Mandelson?" he asked quizzically. "What are they really doing in Millbank Tower? I reckon they're making Mandelsons up there and getting ready to store them in that Millennium dome over there in Greenwich. When the clock strikes midnight on 31st December 1999, millions of Mandelsons will emerge from the dome and civilisation as we know it will be at an end."

Banks is widely regarded as one of the wittiest and most independent of parliamentarians. How long before the Minister for Sport is airbrushed out of the official team photograph?

The professionalising of politics is a depressing trend of our times. The number of MPs who have lived almost totally one-dimensional political lives since a young age is really scary. With the media waiting to pounce on any so-called "gaffes" and magnify indiscreet (or honest) remarks into crises of global proportions, these political clones become ever more guarded and and ever more tedious.

The slow, silent, zombiefication of modern political life

is all about control. Only the high heid yins are allowed to speak, and they seldom have anything truly interesting to say. The great unwashed aren't allowed to speak at all, and if they do speak and get it "wrong", they are put on the toxin drip. If that doesn't work, de-selection looms. In desperation, journalists write profiles of other journalists known as "spin-doctors". This is as incestuous as it gets.

Politics should be a passionate calling. We need more men and women with a genuine non-political "hinterland" – but such people are unlikely to want to sacrifice their thinking life to the demands of some totally politicised boko. The more the centralising control freaks take charge, the less attractive politics becomes to the man or woman of independent mind.

If this scenario were to be replicated at Holyrood, the results would be disastrous. Can Scotland find an antidote to the toxins of the UK political puffer fish?

Blown away by the flute

The seas are heavy in the Pentland Firth, and I am lying down in the swaying ship, eyes closed, like Jonah. It will only take two and a half hours, passing through the Flow to avoid the worst of the storm. (The doom scenario is to be within sight of Scrabster and then to have to turn back. At that stage, death seems like a welcome friend.)

The destination is the great city of London, a place on another planet. It feels very far away. In fact, right now Thurso seems very far away. But we get there, then wait for the train to Inverness. Eight hours later, we are on the London sleeper – my wife and I are taking advantage of a *Herald* two-for-the-price-of-one return deal.

By 7.30 the following morning, we are walking the streets of gold. We will have a few hours in the capital, get back on to the sleeper, then prepare to meet the Pentland Firth again. But enough of that.

We are here for our daughter's graduation. It's been a long journey for her, too. It was while she was working as a waitress in a Kirkwall bar that Fiona decided that she wanted to be a musician. She was taking a year out from school when the revelation came. It was like switching on a light.

She turned down a place at Edinburgh University and did Higher Music instead. A two-year HND music course followed, and then she won a place at Trinity College, London. Four years of enormously hard work saw her gain an honours degree in music. So this is her big day, and we are here for it.

As we make our way to St John's in Smith Square, where the graduation will take place, I reflect on where Fiona got her musical gifts from. I think – modestly of course – of my own distinguished musical career.

The meteoric rise began at the age of 16, with the purchase of a saxophone. I remember how I gazed admiringly at myself in the mirror, and thought I looked really cool. For the first week, I blew, and blew and blew. My face was puce, the veins were sticking out all over my wee Fife heid, but not a sound came out. Not a squeak. At the end of the week, I sought help. I learned how to use my hot lips, baby.

The sound that emerged was truly awesome. It was our neighbours' turn to seek help. My mother claimed that she could hear the scarifying wail over a mile away. Terrified dugs ran for cover. The good people of Cowdenbeath thought it was an unearthly harbinger of some unspeakable doom. There are those still living who have barely recovered. They talk of it even yet in West Fife, in whispers.

At the end of the second week, full of representations and petitions signed by the neighbours, I received a brusque ultimatum: either the sax goes, or you go. I thought about stalking out theatrically, blowing the instrument in defiance, moving heroically on to a fabled career against all the odds; then I remembered that I liked my mammy's cooking and a roof over my head. The sax was returned.

I was not to be outdone, though. Innate musical talent will out. I turned to the banjo. I learned three chords, which was all one needed for a musical career in those days.. Some friends and I formed a band called "The Saints All-

Star Rhythm Group".

This was no ordinary group. We wore luminous painted bowler hats. One of our best numbers was "Tiger Rag", and at the end of each phrase, we each crossed and uncrossed our legs at top speed. Clever, eh? The rise of our band coincided with a sudden, brief, fashion for music in between films at the cinema. We sold out the Lochgelly Cinema de Luxe, and the band went down a treat. Our smouldering sexuality had people in the audience screaming, and the odd corset was thrown on stage.

We were on a roll. We were invited to play on television. My banjo teacher was snoozing in front of the box when he suddenly saw this eerily familiar figure on screen, making a small fortune while playing only three chords. He immediately went back into a coma, from which he has never properly emerged.

The Saints All-Star Rhythm Group was an idea whose hour had come, and it went fairly quickly. Our last gig was at the Gray Park Guild, the West Fife equivalent of oblivion.

Musical talent must keep re-asserting itself, though. I was determined to be a star. Ever resilient and versatile, I turned next to the harmonica. My mouth-organ career took off to the extent that I now play with some folk musicians in a pub in Kirkwall; I also perform with a band called "Jumping John Knox and the Calvinists", with yours truly as JJK (pause while my once-optimistic theological professors cut their throats.) Our first public gig was at the annual general meeting of Arthritis Care.

Do not be dismissive. Who knows, there might have been an agent in the audience. After all, that's how Mozart got started – playing his own compositions in village halls. (It's unkind of you to retort that Mozart was only two years old at the time.)

Anyway, I'm sure that this is where my daughter gets

her musical talent from. That's what I'm claiming anyway, despite the fact that my wife plays the recorder in a local music group. If Ally McCoist can claim a goal when he's 100 yards away, surely I can get the credit.

Our youngest son plays electric guitar and drums (for some reason he has turned down my luminous bowler hat), and the older boy plays the ghetto blaster, loudly. Even the dog plays the xylophone. Hey, this is beginning to sound like the von Trapp family! Soon we'll have nuns cascading up and down the hillsides.

Anyway....my daughter is on stage now, playing the flute with a Chamber Orchestra called *Concilium.* Then she gets her degree scroll; and I'm proud of her. One day, she'll be interviewed on the telly and asked where she gets her talent from, and.....

Now we're back at Scrabster, ready to get on the St Ola. The seas are turbulent. Prepare to meet thy dinner. I hope the boat's on time: I have to play another Jumping John Knox gig. And there might be an agent in the audience.

The hatred that will be the death of us

The drive out of Kirkwall is quite spectacular in the evening light. These June evenings are breathtaking, and each bend in the road reveals a new vista of expansive sky and sea. The bus is heading southwards, towards the first of the Churchill Barriers. We catch sight of our destination – a small chapel, fragile and tiny against the immense backdrop of elemental sights. The busload of pilgrims have come to this place to celebrate the life of a truly remarkable man.

To understand why people of all persuasions have come to a requiem mass for a man who has died in his native Italy at the age of 88, it is necessary to journey back in spirit to Orkney in 1943. One has to picture over 600 Italian prisoners-of-war, captured in North Africa, trudging along the Orkney skyline to Camp 60.

They had been sent to Orkney to work on the Churchill Barriers, a massive series of concrete causeways which seal the eastern approaches to Scapa Flow. Camp 60 consisted of a series of huts. The prisoners planted flowers and made concrete paths, until the whole area was transformed. In their spare time they built a theatre, and a recreation hut which included in its equipment a concrete billiard table.

One thing the men wanted, though, was a chapel. Permission was granted. Late in 1943, two nissen huts were joined together. A sanctuary was built at the far end. The altar, altar rail and holy water stoop, were moulded in concrete. These men worked with a passion; Bruttapasta, a cement worker. Palumbo, a blacksmith. Primavera and Micheloni, electricians. Barcagolini, Fornasier, Pennisi, Sforza and the rest were willing hands. They scavenged for tin cans. Wood for the tabernacle came from a wrecked ship. Two candelabra and a beautiful rood-screen were made by Palumbo, who had been a wrought-iron worker in America. For the entrances on either side of the sanctuary, gold curtains were paid for out of the prisoners' welfare fund.

The man whose vision it was, Domenico Chiocchetti, painted a beautiful picture above the altar – *The Madonna of Peace.* It was based on a holy picture he had carried on his person all through the war. The lovely sanctuary made the rest of the nissen huts look scruffy, and the camp commandant, who got completely caught up in the project, managed to get enough plasterboard to line the whole building. Chiocchetti transformed the interior by his artistry. Then a facade was erected at the front. In the archway, Pennisi moulded in red clay a head of Christ, with a crown of thorns. When the chapel was practically finished, a special service was held, incorporating – with gramophone records in the vestry – the bells and choir of St Peter's, Rome.

In Spring 1945, the prisoners left Orkney, leaving behind causeways linking the southern islands, as well as the legacy of a beautiful chapel. One man stayed on to finish the baptismal font – Domenico Chiocchetti. When it was finished and the war was finally over, he returned home to Italy.

Orkney, largely Protestant, took the Catholic chapel to

its heart. A preservation committee was formed. In 1960, after extensive inquiries, Chiocchetti was traced to his home in Moena, a village in the Dolomites. He made an emotional visit to Orkney, and restored some of the artistic work in the chapel. Before returning home, Domenico wrote to the people of Orkney, "The chapel is yours, for you to love and preserve. I take with me to Italy the remembrance of your kindness and wonderful hospitality. I shall remember always, and my children shall learn from me to love you. I thank all those.....who have given me the joy of seeing again the little chapel of Lambholm where I, in leaving, leave a part of my heart."

Now that great heart has stopped. His frail but serene widow Maria sits with her grown-up family at the front of the chapel, beside the chancel which her dear husband had created in a time of war. As the requiem prayers are said, we think of those days, more than 50 years ago, when these rough-handed, cursing journeymen, with photographs of their loved ones in their pockets, made, out of scraps, something beautiful for God.

Madonna of Peace: created by a reconciling Catholic who has taught us all something from the heart: now lovingly preserved by a Protestant artist, a member of the congregation of St Magnus Cathedral. As the bus heads back towards Kirkwall, I think of a new trail of people on a horizon far from home, the displaced ones of Kosovo.

Hatred will be the death of us all. There must be other ways, as humanity orders Millennial drinks in the last-chance saloon. Crossing the Churchill Barrier, which once echoed to the shouts of Italian prisoners, I look back at the vulnerable little chapel against the background of the ever-changing light of the Orcadian sky: and I understand with my heart, as well as with my mind, that there are precious gifts of spirit which no coinage on earth can buy.

The end is nigh, so don that Armageddon Bra now!

The end of the world is nigh! A Japanese lingerie firm is selling a bra which gives the wearer an early warning system about the end of the world. Called the Armageddon Bra, it is equipped with a sensor that alerts its wearer to incoming missiles. It has a further sensor on the shoulder to warn of objects falling from the sky. Its instructions say, "For more efficient operation, the Armageddon Bra should be worn without outer garments."

As one who doesn't normally wear a bra, I feel this is a form of discrimination against men. Why should women get all the early warnings? Why should they be first to know about incoming missiles? Why should they alone be able to dive for cover when the sensor tells them dangerous stuff is falling from the sky? Why are there no Armageddon Y-fronts? And if men approach burdz who are wearing no outer garments, simply and innocently to get the latest news about Armageddon or to find out from the sensor how Cowdenbeath are getting on, they will be accused of harassment. "Sometimes it's hard to be a man."

The advent of the year 2000 is bringing all kinds of Millennial madness, and this column – without outer garments – can guarantee you that it will increase. We will experience more and more Pre-Millennial Tension, transvestism and hysteria as we move towards the overhyped end of the year of Our Lord 1999. Starey-eyed people are liable to jump out of all sorts of places, with their prophecies about the end of the world. Some seriously demented heidbangers are heading for Israel, even as you read this.

It's important to keep the heid. This prediction game has been going on for aeons. About two centuries after Christ, a group of zealots in Jerusalem thought the world was coming to an end. They climbed to the top of Masada – a place where Jewish martyrs had once committed suicide rather than submit to the enemy – and awaited the End. Well, it came. They all died of sunstroke. So if you're going to gather for the End on top of a mountain, wear at least Factor 25, or it will become a self-fulfilling prophecy. (Which reminds me of a Billy Connolly sketch in which a man goes into the pharmacy and asks for Factor 50. "Sir, that's a bandage," replies the chemist.)

Bishop Gregory of Tours, who was around in the 6th century, thought the end of the world would come between 799 and 806. At the time of the first Millennium, all kinds of groups headed for the hills and the caves. They then had to come back home sheepishly and get on with the rest of their lives.

A man called Joachim of Fiore, a very highly regarded 12th century prophet, predicted the end would come in the year 1260. At the time of the Reformation, the Mayor of Munich was so concerned about rumours of the Second Coming that he had all his crates of booze buried under the ground. In 1532, one of Martin Luther's followers, a minister and amateur mathematician called Michael Stiefel, predicted that the world would end on 9th October, 1533 at precisely 8am. Early that day, the local peasants assembled at his church to await the End. After the deadline passed by some hours, they seized and bound the minister and dragged him off to the local magistrate, where he was sued for damages. One religious woman, Lady Hester Stanhope, always kept two Arab horses in her stable – one for herself and another for the Messiah.

Most prophets have been careful to predict an endgame date well into the future, but others have been foolish enough to predict a time within their own lifetime. This presents obvious credibility problems. The Jehovah's Witnesses have had several cracks at it, and can boast a 100 per cent failure record. This is a case of having your Millennial cake and eating it, over and over again.

Most of the people making the predictions do so by multiplying obscure numbers in the Old Testament, and coming to the conclusion they first thought of. Using this same method, I could predict, for instance, that Cowdenbeath will win the European Cup in 2097, knowing that I will not be proved wrong in my lifetime. (If it did happen, I would expect to be exhumed and beatified immediately, and my relics – transported reverently to holy shrines throughout Europe – would have the power to cure pilgrims of their hæmorrhoids.) Or you could find the number 666 in somebody's telephone number in Bonkle, discover that the person's name is Dewar, and deduce from that fact that Donald is the Mad Apocalyptic Beast of Garscadden predicted by some havering eejit in a cave in Auchenshoogle in 853 BC

Interestingly enough, when Jesus was asked about the day and the hour, he said he didn't have a scooby, or words to that effect. He simply asked that people live lives of accountable readiness. But he wasn't wearing an Armageddon Bra at the time, was he?

To sleep with kings and crofters

The ancient, windswept graveyard of Iona looks out to the fateful stretch of water which separates the holy isle from its much bigger neighbour, Mull. Set beside the restored medieval abbey, the Reilig Oran is earthly home to a number of Scottish, Norwegian, Irish and French kings.

Iona had been regarded as holy ground since the sixth century, when the legendary Irish prince-monk Columba arrived in a coracle on a penitential journey. Columba's Celtic community soon attracted pilgrims from all over Europe.

The great and the bad wanted burial on Iona in the wistful hope that when the last trump sounded and the dead rose from their graves, it might be possible to hang on to the coat-tails of the saints. Some of the grizzly Scottish kings, like Macbeth and Duncan, knew they would need all the help they could get on the day of judgement.

And, of course, in more recent times, John Smith was interred in that same island graveyard. The man who seemed destined to be prime minister is buried beside an island crofter, Donald "Doodie" McFadyen.

Doodie was one of the nicest people I have ever known. He had a stammer, a three-legged dog that followed his tractor round the island, a brilliant sense of humour, and a wonderful kindness. I visited him in hospital just before he died of cancer at a grievously early age, and that same kindness had not deserted him. All his concern was for his wife Jane, and his only son, Logie.

To say that Jane, a quiet, resilient Orcadian woman, was helped by other islanders is an understatement. Men who had more than enough to do rallied round and took it in turns to do the heavy work. Young Logie, who had the same characteristics as his beloved father, took over the croft after he had finished his schooling at Oban. He had to grow up quickly.

When I heard the awful radio news flash early on Sunday, I feared to think who might be involved. As the tragedy unfolded, the news got worse and worse. Logie was missing. So was young Davie Kirkpatrick, a hardworking fisherman whose grandfather was killed while working on the restoration of Iona Abbey; and Ally Dougall, a bright and sunny crewmate on the Silver Spray. Robert Hay, another popular young man, was already dead.

What can one say about this unspeakable event? I knew these fine young men, who had everything to live for. My children were at Iona school with them. The dead men came from salt-of-the-earth families I had got to know and admire; as does Pal Grant, the sole survivor. The situation can only be viewed through tears of sadness.

For young people on Iona to have a wider social life it is necessary to cross over to Mull. The Sound of Iona is their motorway – like crossing the Erskine bridge or the Forth bridge.

Many people's initial explanation on hearing the news of the tragedy was probably in terms of irresponsible youngsters under the influence of drink. They were, in fact, experienced boatmen who had themselves ferried people across that stretch of water countless times.

Iona, like Orkney, is an elemental place. To live on an island is to be continually aware of the fragility of human life, and the formidable power of the elements. It is to be truly conscious of darkness and light. It is to be brought up close against both the bleakness and glory of the human condition.

The Celtic tradition of Iona is full of prayers about journeys:

Relieve thou, O God, each one
In suffering on land or sea,
In grief or wounding or weeping,
And lead them to the house of thy peace this night.

There is much grief and woundedness and weeping on Iona as the island mourns its lost sons. I have stood at too many freshly dug young graves to even attempt to offer cheap comfort. The truth is that the death of a child is not something one "gets over". To get through the days and nights is hard enough – to live with constant loss and pain: to learn to be carried by loving friends: to hang on by the fingernails to improbable ledges of faith.

The season of the year makes the tragedy all the more poignant. A compassionate police officer said on television that for the islanders, Christmas is cancelled. We all knew what he meant. There is such bleakness: and as I write this, cruise missiles are raining down on Baghdad, and the bodies of the young men still lie in the seas around Iona.

And yet – it is very hard to utter any of this without sounding like a grotesque parody of a bad Late Call – the sentimental Christmas should be cancelled, but not the elemental one. The flickering light of Advent is a faint, vulnerable thing, but it somehow refuses to allow the overwhelming blackness to snuff it out totally.

As candles are lit in the darkness at watchnight services throughout the land, the haunting words of a Gaelic poet, Mary Macdonald of Bunessan – the village on Mull where the young men went to a dinner-dance that fateful night – will be sung:

Child in the manger,
Infant of Mary;
Outcast and stranger,
Lord of all!

These words should be articulated while holding the wounded community of Iona in heart and mind. My prayer is that the broken bodies of the missing men will soon be brought home. Then they can be borne in silence to the Reilig Oran, to sleep with the kings and crofters.

Deep Peace of the running wave to you.
Deep Peace of the flowing air to you.
Deep Peace of the quiet earth to you.
Deep Peace of the shining stars to you.
Deep Peace of the Son of Peace to you.